— Nicole Mantzikopoulou —

Why hasn't anyone told me?

The success factors we were never taught

true-me
BREAKTHROUGH COACHING

Including **workbook** for practical exercising

Why Hasn't Anyone Told Me?

The Success Factors We Were Never Taught

Nicole Mantzikopoulou

BALBOA
PRESS
A DIVISION OF HAY HOUSE

Why hasn't anyone told me?
Original Title: Γιατί δεν μου το είπε κανείς; Author: Nicole
Mantzikopoulou Translated by: Marianna Avouri
Art Direction: Antonis Birmpas

Balboa Press books may be ordered through booksellers or by contacting:

Balboa Press
A Division of Hay House
1663 Liberty Drive
Bloomington, IN 47403
www.balboapress.com
1 (877) 407-4847

Print information available on the last page.

ISBN: 978-1-5043-8395-0 (sc)
ISBN: 978-1-5043-8396-7 (hc)
ISBN: 978-1-5043-8641-8 (e)

Library of Congress Control Number: 2017912648

Balboa Press rev. date: 08/24/2017

DEDICATION

To George Nikiforos and Alexander, for inspiring me
to break free from conventionality and seek for true
meaning, authenticity and greatness.

TABLE OF CONTENTS

FOREWORD ————————

by Christy Whitman

Become an observer of those around you, and you'll realize that most of the world is responding to challenging circumstances by attempting to control people and conditions outside of themselves. And yet, this belief that other people and situations hold the power to make us happy or unhappy contradicts a powerful and long-overlooked spiritual truth; a truth which is at the very basis of this book: Whenever we're experiencing struggle or discontent in any aspect of our lives – whether it's in relation to our physical wellbeing, our finances, careers, self-expression or personal relationships – the discontent that we perceive as being caused by outside forces is always an indication of a lack of alignment within ourselves.

Why Hasn't Anyone Told Me provides a much-needed wake-up call from the disempowering belief that we are the passive witness of the reality that surrounds us, and guides us back into the understanding that at every moment of every day, we are the active creators of our own lives.

If you are not yet familiar with the Universal laws that govern deliberate creation, this book will give you a broad basis of understanding about the ways these forces are already at work in your life. And if you're already a practiced deliberate creator, Nicole's approach will take you deeper still by guiding you to more powerfully align and direct the energy that you bring to each situation and interaction. In either case, Why Hasn't Anyone Told Me will remind you that you exist as the powerful center point of every event and circumstance that unfolds in your life.

Nicole Mantzikopoulou is a graduate of the Quantum Success Coaching Academy, which I founded nearly a decade ago to offer a comprehensive training program for certifying Law of Attraction coaches. This book is a distillation of the wisdom Nicole gained as the result of ten years of spiritual searching, and is presented in language that is personal, practical, and easy to apply.

true me

The insights and practices shared throughout these pages will guide you, steadily and surely, to become the deliberate creator you intended to be. Everything that unfolds around you is a reflection of the vibration you are offering, and you are the source of that frequency.

Christy Whitman
Montreal, Quebec
Canada
Fall, 2015

FOREWORD ——————————

by the Author

I have always believed that no matter who we are—no matter what our origin, our education, or profession—regardless of our values, convictions and experiences, we are all likely, sooner or later in our lifetime, to reach a turning point. If I were to give a definition, I would say that turning point is the exact moment when we feel that if nothing changes right away we are in the face of death. Obviously, I am not referring to a natural death but to a most certain spiritual and emotional demise; when our everyday life seems so trivial or so hard that we no longer wish to stay on this path.

On a personal level, this moment came twelve years ago when everything around me seemed to fall apart: marriage, work, family. Everything I had ever built and all that I ever thought was true came crashing down, in a matter of months. I was so shocked by the recurrent mishaps and setbacks that I had no other choice but to switch to survival mode, so as to be able to handle the situations in the best way possible. However, my wounds were deep and I felt as if they kept following me in every step that I took; in the same way that chains tail after a convict.

Trying to overcome the initial shock I decided to look for all kinds of books, CDs, or personal development material readily available. In time, I was able to find some answers to my questions and become more optimistic. Needless to say, it took a great deal of time and effort to be able to systematically apply this newly acquired information, but I finally succeeded in escaping this ongoing recycling of non-productive thoughts and emotions.

However it was not until I received the information—that you now have in hand—that I really felt as though a huge window opened up in my mind to help me gain insight of the way things work in the universe, and therefore in my life. All of a sudden, everything took on a new meaning and for the first time I felt that I had reached my destination; I had arrived at the core of knowledge that I yearned for. Much of this information may have also reached you, one way or another. The purpose of this book is to help you productively synthesize that information and systematically apply it, in order to drastically change your behavior and thus positively alter the result.

If you have never before come into contact with such information, you will probably find it easy-to-understand, but difficult to use. For some people, it may also prove hard to comprehend. For it not only goes beyond our common way of thinking—dictated by our environment, but it also invalidates certain widely-accepted and established action strategies.

Regardless of your initial perceptions, if you gain insight in the information presented in this book, comprehend it and accept it as truthful, it will lead you beyond the conventional and onto a new sphere of thinking which will, in turn, reveal a new sphere of results. You will be in a position to engage your talents and infinite capabilities to attain seemingly-hopeless goals. You will also be able to create a new path of life which will bring you joy, a sense of meaning and completeness.

This book will provide you with the possibility of reaching various levels of comprehension and practical use. One thing is for certain though: you will never be the same person again.

Thank you for giving me the opportunity to be your guide in the path of personal development of your mind and soul.

Nicole Mantzikopoulou
Athens, Greece

Introduction

We all want to make our dreams come true; to create the life that we desire. Some people actually manage to achieve a few goals by engaging into widely-accepted growth strategies, such as education and hard work. Others, however, may have to give up their soul's desire for the sake of safety and stability. And yet, making compromises and restricting our desires are what society considers being indications of maturity. In the same way that society sees a man's complacency as nothing more than a normal consequence. Given that most people around us have had similar experiences, we are falsely led to believe that this is what life is about, or if nothing else, the life that we were born into.

If that is so, how come some people actually manage to realize their dreams and climb up the ladder of success, exceeding even their own expectations? In what way is their behavior different from ours and what has made all that possible?

The answer is both simple and complex. The ones who do succeed are likely to handle even the most difficult situations in an efficient, productive manner. Whether on a conscious or subconscious level, those people are aligned with their desires and the laws of the universe. They have a life philosophy that supports and guides them in their path towards success.

This book aims at sharing these rules with you; handing you over the map that will reveal the treasure that will ultimately change your lives. To teach you the Laws of the Universe that will help you create anything that you desire.

These laws are not a recent discovery. They have been here since the beginning of time. Their power is repeatedly reflected in the preaching of many leading spiritual teachers and philosophers, such as Buddha and Jesus Christ, and in the words of Plato and Aristotle. However, they have been communicated to us in a fragmented or incomplete manner, much like a puzzle whose pieces have been scattered through time. It is therefore impossible to perceive them, to understand and apply them.

Whether or not we are aware of them and whether or not we choose to use them, the Laws of the Universe exist. Although they are not dependent on our behaviors, these rules apply and set the legal-structural balance of the world in which we live in. In order to understand their meaning, just think of the Law of Gravity who is always in effect, without exceptions and regardless of our awareness.

Every time you throw an object upwards, you know with certainty that it will return to earth, as gravity comes into place. Our whole lives are organized in a way that takes this law as a given, and depend on its undisputed power. That is also the way that the other laws of the universe work. However, since they are basically unknown to us, we have never planned our behaviors according to their axes and, as a result, our lives are still far from being harmonious, balanced and gratifying.

These laws function with precise, predictable and unwavering certainty. They make no distinctions. Regardless of age, upbringing, religion, origin, education, gender, or financial standing, the laws operate in their entirety on a permanent and continuous basis, both on a conscious and a subconscious level.

On the other hand, the fact that you ignore these laws is probably the reason why you experience the things you do: sickness, unfulfilling relationships, debt, job-related frustration, etc.

When unaware of the laws, it is unlikely that you will get to win the game. Instead, you may find yourself playing into the hands of others who apply them, deliberately or not.

Knowing these rules will convince you that there are no lucky or unlucky people. There are merely intentional and unintentional creators. If you insist on believing in luck, you must admit that even luck can only last for so long: a moment, a day, or maybe a week. If, on the other hand, someone's experiences are consistently positive, it is made apparent that this person has aligned himself or herself with the laws of the universe. By reading this book you will also come to realize that.

The Laws of the Universe—otherwise called Laws of Creation, or Laws of Nature— are constant and fixed principles governing the entire universe.

That is to say, they are the means by which our world continues to sustain itself and grow.

Understanding these laws will give you a significant edge, as it is a prerequisite for learning the rules of life. Moreover, the knowledge of these rules will help you form the relationships you want, gain more money, get a new job, or even manage to detoxify from negative situations and emotions, such as anxiety, disappointment, and depression.

Most people are not aware of these laws and therefore cannot apply them in order to create the kind of life they want. By learning these laws, you will literally be able to attract abundance, success, freedom, and joy, with considerably less effort.

Instead of trying to find happiness and abundance in a constant struggle for the best—always in search of more work-hours or more material goods—you just have to learn how to flow in unity with the laws to bring balance into your life. There is absolutely no reason why you should lead a life where you always feel overwhelmed, exhausted, unsatisfied, anxious, and scared. Because that is what happens when your actions resist the natural laws and the universe, in turn, creates imbalance in your efforts.

For you reading this book, one thing can prove to be a challenge: coping with possible thoughts of uncertainty or doubt regarding the validity of the information listed herein. In the event that something like that comes up, it will only be on account of the huge gap that exists between the material in hand and that what you have been taught; which dictates the actions that you think you should take in order to bring results. You may also be concerned about the fact that you will have to give up behaviors which are admittedly counterproductive, but are however very familiar to you and form the foundation of what you consider to be your identity. Such thoughts might make the process a difficult one.

Nevertheless, you should not be discouraged. Doubt and uncertainty are basically two very natural, biological reactions to anything new or different. They result from our subconscious need for stability that ensures our present lifestyle; even when that lifestyle falls short of our potential. Usually, doubt and uncertainty are merely the aftereffects of our fear of the unknown. Or, they can also derive from our own disbelief in our abilities and our personal value to successfully take on this new and unknown path.

The way to deal with this challenge is to continue reading. This will send a clear message to yourself: that you are ready to find new answers to your questions, to test new strategies and try doing things differently. Do not be afraid to question your own doubt and try to keep an open mind so as to fully grasp the information. You have already taken the first step by reading these lines.

In addition to the information laid out in this book, you will be presented with a Work-book, filled with exercises, processes, and statements that will help you practice what you have learned and realize its potential power. By consciously applying the laws and through consistent training, you will make the transition; from a life of anxiety to a life of knowledge, from a life of struggle to a life of victory, and from a life of deprivation to a life of abundance.

So let us begin our exciting journey that will change the way you see the world. It is my hope that you will rise above your current consciousness and reach new levels of enlightenment and success that will bring you closer to recognizing your true identity and your infinite potential.

Chapter 1
THE LAW OF ATTRACTION

We are the creators of our lives.
It is our thoughts and our
emotions that attract our
experience.

QUANTUM SCIENCE AND RECENT THEORIES

Quantum Physics and Quantum Mechanics have made significant discoveries over the years. They have produced a great number of questions and have provided us with new hypotheses and possible interpretations of how the Universe works and, therefore, how do our lives. In this book, we will only concern ourselves with the cornerstone theory that they offer:

EVERYTHING IN THE UNIVERSE IS ENERGY

- All things—visible and invisible—when divided into their most basic forms, their basic subatomic structures, are nothing but energy. An energy that has its own vibration and frequency.
- As this energy is emitted to the environment—the Universe—it attracts energies of similar frequency or vibration.

It is not the purpose of this book to cite this knowledge in a scientific manner. For those of you who are interested in further exploring these disciplines, there are some recommended readings at the end of the book.

In case, however, you would like to comprehend how these things apply to your daily lives, you may want to try the following, well-known, experiment: use a dropper to pour a drop of oil on a given surface. Next, try to pour a drop of water on top of it. What will happen? The oil will repel the water. Why is that? Because even though both oil and water are liquid components, these two masses—in their basic subatomic form—have different structures and different energy vibrations. Therefore, they cannot attract each other. They cannot mix. Conversely, if you pour a drop of oil over another drop of oil, the two drops will mix because their molecular structure is the same, much like their vibration and emitted energy.

Things become more interesting when we apply that theorem to human reality, to affirm that all things are energy; our thoughts, our emotions, even this book that you are now reading. According to Quantum Physics, these measurable energy frequencies or vibrations are constantly being projected on the environment in exchange for energies of similar frequencies or resonance. These energies are expressed in the physical world in the form of thoughts, emotions, and situations that we attract into our lives. In other words, the frequency with which our own energy vibrates affects our life experiences.

If all this seems somewhat incomprehensible, do not worry. The only thing you need to understand is that everything is energy, including you. It is your energy vibration that determines the results you bring into your life.

Think of the following sequence:

Convictions ➤ thoughts ➤ emotions = energy ➤ results

Every conviction gives rise to a thought and every thought gives rise to an emotion that has a direct and profound effect on your own frequency or energy field. When the thought is of a positive nature, it affects the quality of your personal frequency and generates positive emotions. Likewise, a negative thought evokes negative feelings. Much like a radio's signal, the frequency of your vibration is then transmitted to the universe. The universe, in turn, responds by attraction: by sending us people, situations and experiences that are aligned with the specific frequency. In other words, the energy that we emit—based on what we think and feel—is the phenomenon that creates the events and situations that arise daily in our experiences.

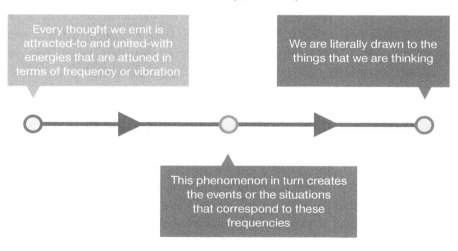

Every thought we emit is attracted-to and united-with energies that are attuned in terms of frequency or vibration

We are literally drawn to the things that we are thinking

This phenomenon in turn creates the events or the situations that correspond to these frequencies

DEFINITION OF THE LAW OF ATTRACTION

Building on these theories of Quantum Physics, the Law of Attraction was formulated. According to this law:

> **Everything that is transmitted to the outer universe is united with (attracts or is attracted by) energies that are of equal resonance, frequency or vibration**

This means that anything you emit into the universe—in the form of thoughts, emotions, or subsequent actions—is united with thoughts, emotions, and results that correspond exactly to those energy frequencies.

Let us examine an everyday example: While you are watching the national financial report on TV, you begin to worry about the future and you become overwhelmed with fear and anxiety. You later discuss the issue with your friends, but you end up feeling even worse. When the utility bills come, your feeling of discomfort grows. You go on a trip and you get a flat tire, and this unforeseen expense stresses you even more. Your financial distress is overpowering and you are deeply concerned about the future.

Now look at the opposite example: You meet someone special and the love game begins. The very thought of seeing her makes your heart beat fast. You feel positive, motivated and full of energy. You have nothing but love and compassion for others. The news about your country's economic situation is of no interest to you. What you are experiencing is exciting and each day seems brighter than the one before. You feel all-powerful, attractive, loving, and magnanimous. Life is beautiful and every moment bears a gift.

What do these two situations have in common? Both attest to the fact that a single thought or emotion attracts or unites with similar thoughts and emotions that will, in turn, shape the experiences that correspond to them.

What is the difference between them? Their difference lies in the quality of vibration being emitted or attracted. Since anxiety is a low vibration, it produces physical discomfort, whereas love—a high energy vibration— induces motivation, exuberance and joy. These significantly different vibrational states are emitted into the universe: unnoticed, yet powerful. They attract experiences and life events that reflect similar high or low energy vibrations. The degree to which you enjoy economic abundance, job satisfaction, meaningful relationships, vitality and well-being—all the results that you bring into your life today—conveys information regarding the quality of energy you emit into the universe. Each experience, at the time it occurs, is a direct reflection of the energy that you send out. That is the essence of the Law of Attraction and the secret behind every creation.

SPIRITUAL REFERENCES TO THE LAW OF ATTRACTION

The Law of Attraction is, by no means, a new concept. For centuries, the great spiritual leaders of mankind spoke of these truths, references of which can also be found throughout the Holy Scriptures.

> Matthew 7:7, "…Whatever you seek when you pray,
> believe that it will be given to you and it will."

Here, there is a reference to the first part of the law. You must first identify what it is that you desire and then ask for it. If you believe that you will receive it, you will. It is unlikely that anything else will happen.

> Luke 17:6, "The Lord answered, "if you had faith even as small as a
> mustard seed, you could say to this mulberry tree, "May you be uprooted
> and thrown into the sea", and it would obey you!"

> Matthew 7:7, "Ask God for the spiritual and material goods
> that you need and they will be given to you, seek and you
> shall find the good that you desire. Knock on the door of
> divine love and the door shall be opened to you."

Both passages above refer to the power of strong faith that leads to the realization of thoughts and desires. Whichever they are, and as impossible as they may seem to achieve, they will come true; provided that you declare them with strong, genuine faith.

Matthew 13:22, "He, who received the seed that fell among the thorns is the man who hears the word of God, but the worries of his life and the deceitfulness of wealth choke the word, making it unfruitful."

"Faith is the substance of things hoped for and the evidence of things not seen."

Again here, reference is made to the significance of faith. When you ask for something that you want or desire, but—at the same time—question your ability to see it come to life, then your search is fixated, pressured and stressful. It is as if you are searching among the thorns.

Faith is the cornerstone of spirituality. It is an idea-thought that you are confident exists, even if you are not able to prove so. Therefore, every time you have a certain belief, your thoughts support and enhance its existence thus making it part of your experience. In other words, whenever you believe that it is possible to create the things you need and you seek to make them happen, you do. However, when you are stressed and exercise pressure to experience the things that you want, you actually fail to receive them. Because your behavior indicates that you have lost your faith and misunderstood the essence of these words.

Some of Buddha's teachings are similar in nature:

"We are what we think. All that we are arises with our thoughts. With our thoughts, we make the world."

"How a man thinks of himself, is the way he is."

"The thoughts that you focus upon will present themselves in form and create your reality."

Gautama Buddha also preaches:

"All we are is the result of the thoughts we have had. If a man speaks of actions in a devious way, pain will follow."

"If a man speaks of actions with a pure thought, happiness
will follow. Just like the shadow that never leaves him..."

We could list hundreds of references from spiritual teachers and the scriptures.
But again, we would sidetrack from the scope of this book. I do hope that you
have understood their connection and contribution to shaping what we now
call the Law of Attraction.

THE LAW OF ATTRACTION TODAY

The Law of Attraction acquired its name only recently. Nonetheless, its seeds
of consciousness have been planted in many popular expressions such as:
"You reap what you sow," "As you make your bed so you must lie on it," "Like
attracts like," "Where attention goes energy flows," and "What you focus on
expands."

The attribution of all those different names to the law is nothing other than an
attempt to essentially interpret a situation that is beyond explanation; at least
in the context of known physical phenomena. But then again, those names
can be misleading as they fail to recognize the man as creator and deprive
him of his power. Some indicative names and characterizations are: fate, luck,
it was meant to be, in place, karma, coincidence, and synchronicity.

"You reap what you sow"

"As you make your bed
so you must lie on it"

"Like attracts like"

"Where attention goes
energy flows"

"What you focus on
expands"

Fate

Luck

Meant to be

In place

Karma

Coincidence

Synchronicity

The essence of the Law of Attraction, which is primarily the energy interaction
between two objects, is defined as a physical phenomenon and as such
it is taught in the Physics classroom: action-reaction, cause and effect.

However, its application is exclusively restricted to the time-space of our physical dimension and thus our mind is not encouraged—at least within the educational scope—to look for an application in another area.

REALIZING THE EFFECT OF THE LAW OF ATTRACTION ON OUR LIVES

Up to this point, you have learned that your thoughts, emotions, and actions produce energy of specific frequency and vibration which, in turn, attracts thoughts, emotions, and actions of similar energy.

What does that mean? It means that you can attract only the energies that you emit. That is to say, you attract the qualities that you, yourself possess.

If you think of abundance, the energy vibration of that thought is emitted into the environment and results in attracting similar energy vibration (abundance).

The same principle applies to thoughts of deprivation or restriction. When you believe that something that you are currently experiencing is not good enough, you send out its signal and energy vibration, and you unavoidably end up recycling that type of experience. That is because the Law of Attraction always ensures that you consistently receive the things that you think of, in even bigger quantities.

Negative emotions attract negative experiences, even if that was never your intention. In a similar manner, the positive emotions you have—either consciously or subconsciously—attract and bring about positive life experiences. As I mentioned earlier, you can only attract the qualities you possess. For instance, if you wish to experience freedom and joy, you have to transmit the energy and vibration of freedom and joy. By doing so, you will consistently attract such qualities to your life.

This only goes to show you how extremely important it is to be aware of your focus (in the thought process) and your emotional state, at any given moment. It is made apparent that the law makes no distinction and delivers them both: the desirable and the non-desirable, depending on the signal emitted on each occasion.

> Depending on the signal you emit,
> the Law will deliver to you both: the
> DESIRABLE and the NON-DESIRABLE.

The realization that you, yourself attract unwanted situations is extremely important. It is a prerequisite without which you will not be able to make changes to your life. In case you are wondering how to make it happen, let me tell you that it is fairly easy, once you really understand the way that the Law of Attraction works. From early on in life, you have been trained to take notice, concentrate, and talk about the things you do not want. Time and again, you have wallowed in negative thoughts associated with unpleasant situations, i.e. anger, fear, frustration, anxiety, and even deprivation. By focusing your attention on such thoughts and emotions, you actually enhance and empower them. Consequently, you unintentionally create more of those negative situations, because—as already mentioned—the Law of Attraction works nonstop and makes no distinction.

Let us look at the following examples:

If you believe you are overweight, and for this you are unhappy, the very act of discovering and adopting a proactive and positive attitude—that will help you take action in order to create the ideal body and in turn feel fit—is almost impossible. Such efforts, by definition, are opposed to the Law of Attraction.

If again you are frustrated because your business venture has not been successful, it is highly unlikely that the situation will get any better; because improvement in the face of discouragement defies the law.

If you constantly feel angry because someone has taken advantage of you, lied to you, disgraced you, or stolen from you, there is absolutely nothing you can do to stop the recycling of these situations because that would once more contradict the law.

It is, therefore, really important that you learn to observe your thoughts and emotions, so that you do not end up attracting the things you do not want. Only then, will you get a real head start. Even better, if you learn to direct your thoughts and emotions towards the positive things that you want to experience. But we are going to refer to that in greater detail in a later section.

REBUTTAL OF FALSE ACTION-STRUCTURES

The Law of Attraction also reveals another important truth about the way that our world functions, which again contradicts what we have learned so far.

The modern man has been trained to think that in order to "be" someone, he ought to do and own. To that end he studies, he works, and he builds; always being in a state of continuous action. He was taught that, by exhibiting these behaviors, he will get to own a car, a house, friends, connections and money. And that—based on his results—he would be recognized for who he is: a man of worth, capability and accomplishment, or an unworthy and incompetent underachiever.

That is where the greatest deception of mankind lies: in the current structure of our lives and the purpose it serves. That is not the way that the universe works—quite the opposite.

In order to do and to own, you must first BE. And based on who you are, actions and possessions will follow—naturally and without much effort—as the result of existence. According to Quantum rules and the Law of Attraction, in order to attract worthiness, capability and accomplishment to your lives, you need first to embrace their energy and vibration. No action or object—by itself—is likely to have that effect. It is, therefore, easy to understand that this truth defies many values and structures of the modern, basically materialistic, society; while it emphasizes other, more spiritual principles.

Right now you are probably thinking there is only a slim possibility that you could rebut the things that—you were led to believe—have determined your personal value and the quality of your experiences. You may also believe that reversing them is a goal far from your reach. Similarly, you may feel it is highly unlikely that you would be able to later adopt and apply this new knowledge.

However, if you are really interested in shaping a different reality, one that is way more satisfactory than the present one, then give yourself a chance.

Below are two smart pieces of advice that will help you get started and overcome resistance. In the Workbook you will also come across similar processes and tools.

- 🔑 Let the power of faith help you. Think about what you want to experience and show faith in your ability to bring it to your life. Even if you are not yet sure how to make that happen. From that position, you will be able to draw the strength and the vibration you need to knowingly experiment with the law and eventually change your way of thinking.

- 🔑 In case that fails, you can simply play a game: Pretend that you were cast a role in a show, where you are exactly the person who you want to be. With frequent—daily—repetition, you will be able to align yourself with the character's thoughts and resulting emotions and you will soon become the person you want to be. Since your brain is in no position to distinguish between something that you experience for real and something that is merely a product of your imagination, you will be able to create the desired vibration. And the Law of Attraction will once again work effectively.

APPLYING THE LAW OF ATTRACTION

When you reach the point of acceptance and acknowledgment of the reality of the Law of Attraction, the question is this: is it easy to apply?

If I were to give a simple reply, I would say that –on the condition of our capability for logic—the application of the law is fairly easy.

However, your ability to successfully proceed with properly applying the law is contingent upon your current degree of consciousness. Namely, inasmuch as you know yourself and are aware of the implications of your thoughts and actions. It also depends on your beliefs and values system, the one which has guided your actions up until this moment, for it may hinder your efforts to experiment and train in this new field of thought and action.

To be more specific, you cannot attract one thing into your life, while thinking and feeling the opposite. You cannot, for example, bring abundance into your life when you constantly focus on and transmit thoughts of deprivation, shortage, anxiety, doubt, and criticism. In short, to draw abundance, you must ensure that your thoughts and emotions radiate the energy vibration of abundance. It is very likely that for the better part of your lives, your thoughts have been intrinsically negative. The fact that you have rarely focused on positive thoughts or thoughts of abundance, makes it hard for you to automatically connect with them. It is because of this routine—always maintaining focus on the negative side—that you encounter obstacles in the application of the law. As of now, we will call this routine, a program.

At this point, you may reasonably ask: "Where do thoughts come from?" What are the criteria by which our mind processes an external stimulae, classifies it as positive or negative, and reaches a conclusion that presents itself in the form of a thought? Thoughts result from our convictions about life, about people, and about ourselves. We could even go so far as to say that perception is the outset in the chain of mental and creative processes. As a matter of fact, our brain forms most convictions from the moment of our birth, up until the age of seven. They can relate to almost any fact or condition and they basically reflect the beliefs of the other people in our environment; their notion about what is right or wrong in the world, or in any given situation for that matter. Given the circumstances (our young age), these beliefs are being automatically accepted—no critical thinking involved. As a rule, con- victions are nothing other than repetitive thoughts that carry an emotional weight and, as such, exhibit a great energy intensity and force. They basically function like powerful magnets—with their own vibration and frequency—and they attract congruent situations.

Consider the following example: You live in a country that is undergoing an economic crisis and this causes you to feel fear on a daily basis. Nonetheless, the economic crisis is merely a fact. In reality, your feeling of fear is produced by your beliefs and thoughts on the matter, as well as on your ability to cope with the situation.

If you want to fully understand how you have applied the law so far, take a look around you and take notice of the people, the environment, and the situations you are experiencing. All of them reveal the quality of your beliefs and thoughts. In case you are failing to experience certain desires of yours, perhaps that is because you are upholding a conviction that keeps them from realizing. In other words, it is possible—even though you truly believe you want something—to maintain thoughts that prevent you from experiencing it; without even being aware of it.

If you seek abundance, but deep inside you feel that affluence is the byproduct of immoral acts, or that it requires excessive effort and compromises (that you are not willing to make), every time that you attempt to become more prosperous—beyond what your program stipulates—you will be faced with an inner conflict. Consequently, there is only a small likelihood that you will attain your goal.

The following example is very indicative of what we create when we have no knowledge of the Law of Attraction. Recently, I learned that an acquaintance of mine had financial troubles. Apparently, a property he owned, and for which he received rent, was suddenly vacated by the tenant. As a result, the man suffered the loss of significant monthly revenue. He therefore began to stress and his anxiety grew daily, even though his life in general was going well. It seemed he was unable to cope with the fear—brought about by this economic hardship—and the negative feeling just took over. After a while, his health was affected and he soon had to seek help, as he began showing signs of depression and was often taken ill. It is important to note here that, even though a lot of people had expressed an interest in the property, no one was willing to rent it; despite the fact that its price was a bargain. The months passed, and still there was nothing.

When I finally got to meet with this person, I immediately came to realize the cause of the situation. For some odd reason, the man believed that the property would not be leased before December; he was convinced of that. When I asked him why he would think that, he failed to give me a logical explanation. But I could tell that his conviction was so strong that had literally taken over his mind. The result: the property was rented in the beginning of December! Whereas the man had known and had deliberately applied the Law of Attraction, he would have anticipated that his belief would be substantiated, and manifested in the form of experience. In the meantime, he could have avoided the unnecessary stress, or he could have tried to change his initial belief so that the desired result would come sooner. As it was, he could have spared himself the suffering.

The next example also goes to show you the power of thought. A friend from abroad—who is usually in perfect health—got a viral disease, and although bedridden for over 10 days, she was still not getting any better. I remembered that something similar happened to her the year before, around the same dates, when she had to stay in bed for two weeks. So I asked her if she had observed that too. She gave me a positive response and she also told me that every year, near the time of her birthday, she gets sick. From our discussion, she seemed convinced that everyone gets sick when their birthdays are coming up. That was, she said, a widespread belief in her country. At that point, I realized that my friend—in anticipation of her birthday—somehow programmed her body to be most vulnerable around that time. And as a result, every year, she would be taken ill.

It is important to acknowledge that it is our internal reality—our beliefs, our thoughts and the resulting feelings—which creates our external reality; not the other way around. Safe to say, that our experience is not determined by an economic crisis, an unleased property, or a virus in the environment. In essence, what causes our external experiences is rather the quality and consistency of our convictions: about people, situations and ourselves. Therefore, what our convictions attract and produce are the results we get.

To be able to overcome your present self and the situations you have created in your life, all it takes is focus, discipline, practice, perseverance, and faith in new beliefs and more empowering thoughts. Only in this way, will the Law of Attraction run its course and bring you the result you desire.

You must realize that this new knowledge can support you in radically changing the facts in your life; by handing you a magic wand and making you the creator. If there is something that you do not yet have, you can attract it—systematically and consistently —through the power of thought concentration. According to the law, the very act of focusing on something (a fact, a situation or object) results in your alignment with its energy and the quality of the desired result (fact, situation or object). When that happens, you will be able to bring what you desire into your own reality. Truth be told, there is no magic in this process, it is just the Law of Attraction brought into play.

What actually takes place is that your permanent and steady focus on the desired effect essentially directs your mind to find new paths or possible solutions. That is to say, your mind will generate new ideas and realize new opportunities which will dictate new action on your part, and will therefore bring you new, deliberate and desired results. It is a Law of the Universe in force.

PREPARE YOURSELF TO USE THE LAW EFFECTIVELY

The first step in cooperating with the Law of Attraction is to recognize where you focus your attention. What are the thoughts that occupy your mind? Because whatever constitutes your point of focus, either intentionally or unintentionally, is what you will attract into your life.

To get a sense of things, start by noticing your environment to gain awareness of your present reality. Do you like what you see? Or would you rather have some things improve?

Provided that you observe something that satisfies you, you must make an effort to locate the exact thoughts that have generated that result, because it is in your best interest to maintain these thoughts.

If, on the other hand, you see something that you are not satisfied with, in any or some of the areas in your life, you should not be discouraged. Your present experiences do not dictate how your life will evolve; given that your thoughts may change in the blink of an eye.

It is useful to know that it only takes seventeen seconds for our mind to shift its focus. After that time, you acquire the vibration of your thought and the Law of Attraction goes on to attract yet another similar thought. If you continue along this line, sixty eight seconds suffice to change and stabilize your energy somewhere else. I urge you to try it, right now. Consider, for example, someone with whom you have a beautiful relationship. Maintain this thought for a moment, time yourself for sixty eight seconds, and see how your emotions change; becoming far more pleasurable, enthusiastic and enjoyable.

It stands to reason that if you want to bring about a change in your life, now you know that you must first change the energy you transmit—through your convictions, thoughts and emotions on the matter. To that end, you need to embrace a new conviction, thought, or emotion whose energy vibration is congruent with what you wish to experience.

BARRIERS TO SUCCESSFULLY IMPLEMENTING THE LAW

If, however, during your first attempts to apply the law, you do not get immediate results, I recommend that you keep on training in the higher energy frequency of your newly acquired conviction.

In case you are wondering why you have not yet received what you desire, you must understand that it is not because you are unworthy or not intelligent enough. Nor is it because fate is working against you or someone has beaten you to it. It is merely owed to the fact that you are, deliberately or not, still holding onto a vibration pattern that is inconsistent with the vibration that you want to bring into your life. In short, it is the result of the difference in vibrations: the one you are currently transmitting and the one that relates to the object of your desire.

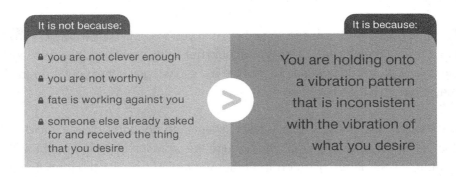

It is not because:

- you are not clever enough
- you are not worthy
- fate is working against you
- someone else already asked for and received the thing that you desire

>

It is because:

You are holding onto a vibration pattern that is inconsistent with the vibration of what you desire

Why is that? Because the most basic function of our mind (our subconscious, in particular) is to sustain us in life. It is because of this biological need for survival, that any attempt to bring about change will automatically be resisted and rendered void. On the assumption that most of us have a deep fear of the unknown, our efforts are more or less destined to fail. You need to understand, that the fact alone that you are breathing satisfies your brain—its purpose has been achieved. That is true, even when you do not live up to your potential or fail to lead a life in accord with your desires. In order to be able to go beyond your mind's maintenance and survival program, you must converse with yourself in a systematic and consistent way. It is important that you are fully aware of what your plans and goals are. Only then, will your mind become your ally. Otherwise, it will continue to be your biggest obstacle.

It is, therefore, very important to realize the size of the discrepancy between the vibrations of what you desire and what you actually transmit. Nothing can be attracted, when thinking and feeling the opposite. For example, you are not in a position to attract the ideal, loving relationship when your mind clings to the fear of loneliness. In a like manner, you may not aspire to abundance, when all that you think about is your debt. And, similarly, you may not hope for the perfect body, when you constantly blame yourself for being overweight. The quality of those negative thoughts and emotions is diametrically opposed to your desire. And, as we have already said, you can only attract situations which are in accord with your thoughts and beliefs.

The Law of Attraction works in a verifiable, unwavering and predictable way; no exceptions made. Only by altering the quality of your beliefs and thoughts, will you be able to change what takes place in your experience. That alone is worth taking the time to locate the beliefs, thoughts, feelings, or actions that prevent you from making the change. The Workbook will further support you in getting the hang of the process.

After you have successfully located those limiting beliefs, the second step is to clearly express what you want to create and why. When you think about what you stand to gain from attaining your goals, you generate positive energy; the energy of happiness, hope, and motivation. This, in turn, brings you closer to your desire. Never forget, that the law is always and constantly in operation. It is up to you to decide to use it—knowingly so—to your advantage, in order to clear the path ahead. In the next chapter, we will discuss the creative process in greater detail.

WHEN IS THE RIGHT TIME TO APPLY THE LAW OF ATTRACTION?

No matter what is going on in your life, now is the time to employ the Law of Attraction.

Bear in mind that, there is not a single thing in your environment that needs to be different for the change to take effect; even if you are the only person who acknowledges the validity of this law. All you have to do is to make the decision and begin immediately. The only change that is required is within you. Having, therefore, understood this law, as well as the other laws that you will find later in the book, once you get started with the process, it will not be long before you succeed in creating the things that you want for yourself.

Plan your new path and stick to it, guided by everything you learn as you read this book. Rest assured you will reach your destination.

I hope, by now, you have started realizing that life is more than a set of situations happening at random. We are all responsible for our lives and it is our vibration that attracts our experiences. In fact, the Law of Attraction will deliver whatever it is we are looking for—with our thoughts and emotions. We must, however, learn to consciously ask for the things we want, so as to tune in to their frequency and allow the law to work in our favor.

In conclusion:

- You have the ability to create your life the way that you want it.

- The powerful Law of Attraction will respond to your every request and vibration (transmitted through your thoughts and emotions), provided that you maintain your focus.

- All it takes is for you to align the vibration of your thought with the vibration of what you want to attract.

Life is more than a set of situations
happening at random

You are responsible for your life and it is your
vibration that attracts your experiences

The Law of Attraction will deliver
to you exactly what you ask for

How do you apply the
Law of Attraction?

Chapter 2
THE LAW OF DELIBERATE CREATION

The deliberate and consistent
focus on the desired is what
leads us to attain it.

DEFINITION OF THE LAW OF DELIBERATE CREATION

In the previous chapter, you learned that whatever thoughts or feelings you transmit; you attract them in the form of situations and objects.

However, in most cases—unless of course you are aware of the Law of Attraction— the vibration you send out is either subconscious or spontaneous. Accordingly, if you happen to notice something that pleases you, it is likely that you will feel joy, happiness, or even delight. Consequently, your positive vibration rises. In the opposite case, where you see something that annoys you, you will emanate the negative vibration of anger and possibly indulge in it; although it will make you feel bad.

With this automatic mechanism in place, whenever you gaze at your favorite work of art you will probably feel pleased. Then again, if you notice trash dumped outside a garbage can, you are likely to feel discontented. There is no right or wrong. You need simply realize that, with every passing second, you transmit a vibration into in the universe; drawing the things that are directly related to this vibration. It is, therefore, in your best interest to transmit what you desire so as to ensure its reception.

This truth is further confirmed by the Law of Deliberate Creation, which urges us to take action and consciously create the things we want in life.

> **That what you are thinking—**
> **you begin to attract**
>
> **That what you are thinking and**
> **feeling—you attract easier**
>
> **That what you are consistently thinking**
> **and feeling—you receive**

At some point in our lives, we have all experienced the joy of being the Deliberate Creator. Try to recall a goal you had once set and managed to attain: forming a relationship with your partner, getting into graduate school, landing a particular job, taking a journey, etc. Now, ask yourself what was it that you did differently then? Is it possible that it had something to do with your strong desire and confidence to succeed, your unwavering focus on the goal, or your disciplined action to attain it?

All of them are regarded as effective thought-and-action strategies. In the same manner, you can achieve any goal that you set. Nothing is out of your reach, provided you believe in it and your action is efficient and systematic. Understanding and recognizing the mechanism which activates every time you express your intention to experience something, is knowledge that gives you a head start in anything you want to accomplish.

THE ADVERSARY OF DELIBERATE CREATION

You must realize that, in the event that you do not take into account the Law of Deliberate Creation, you might as well be running on auto pilot. In other words, you are letting your program (the system of values and convictions that you were exposed to during your childhood) guide you in whatever you want to do. If, by any chance, this program helps you accomplish your goals, then— by all means—keep on applying it, for it benefits you. If, on the other hand, it contains convictions that somehow discourage or weaken you, then those limiting beliefs will easily get in the way of experiencing the things you desire.

In the second case, you have unintentionally assumed the role of the spectator or the observer. Life happens, yet you are on the receiving end. You do not get to shape situations or events; you simply accept them the way that others have shaped them. Although you may not actually realize it, you often operate according to the way you have been trained or accustomed to. You, therefore, react to situations without even going through the thought process. Only when you do decide to take yourself off the automatic pilot and, instead, offer a vibration that positively relates to what you want to create—namely by adopting thoughts and beliefs that are positive and consistent with what you want to experience—will you have successfully applied the Law of Deliberate Creation.

Assume, for example, that you have recently changed jobs and you find yourself investing a lot of time in your new position, trying to establish yourself. At the same time, however, you believe that you will surely encounter someone to oppose you, thus your progress will most possibly be obstructed (that was actually the reason for quitting your three previous jobs). It is highly likely that your job experience will recycle itself this time around, as well. Perhaps, sometime soon, you will face a similar situation which will also make you lose hope, make you feel discouraged, tired and defeated. The presence of this low energy will in fact reduce your productivity and hold you back; you will not be inspired to find and bring into play a strategic action plan that will help you get promoted. But if you change your belief and acknowledge that now is your time; that everyone is supportive and that they all recognize your value and want to reward it, it goes without saying, you will be motivated and inspired. That will raise your vibration, increase your productivity and ultimately bring you the positive results you want.

So you can see that the only condition for becoming a Deliberate Creator is to accept the fact that you live in a vibrating universe and that you, yourself is part of the energy. Once you accept yourself as a vibrating entity, with all the power to create your own experiences, you can embark on the delightful journey of deliberate creation. You will be holding the key that will take you from where you are now to where you want to be.

It is true that, for many of us, the mere thought of our lives in the light of vibrations, seems unusual or even absurd. I believe, though, that the basic function of this phenomenon is very logical. Let us again examine the example of the radio broadcast: sending and receiving signals. As you well know, in order to listen to the station you like, you have to tune in to the frequency of transmission. Similarly, in order to attract what you want, you have to tune in to the frequency of the energy of what you desire. If you have not yet applied the law, it is most probably because you never knew or realized its existence.

In order to successfully apply this knowledge, you must also understand and accept the two basic principles that follow.

WELL-BEING IS THE ONLY ENERGY FLOWING IN THE UNIVERSE

In the previous chapter we said that everything is energy. You must understand that Well-being is the only energy current that is flowing. That is to say, there is only one type of energy in the universe and that is the energy of abundance, wellness, and benevolence. You may flow alongside the energy or resist it; but if you let yourself go with the flow, all is well. If you, instead, get in the way, you may end up in some kind of hardship, i.e. get sick.

As you are reading these lines, you are either flowing with the energy of Well-being, or not. And you can tell by the way that you are feeling. If you feel good, it means you are flowing in the same direction as the universe, but if you feel bad, it is because you are flowing in the opposite direction.

To be able to better understand this analogy, I will now ask you to do the following exercise1: Close your eyes and imagine the following: you are in a boat, rowing against the river. Even though you desperately try to move forward, you cannot do it. You are clearly exhausted. If that is not enough, you are incredibly stressed over the possibility of being drifted away by the current. Now, take a deep breath and let go of the oars and allow the current to slowly turn your boat, bringing it in alignment with the natural flow of the river. Feel the boat moving and changing its course. Then, surrender yourself to the natural flow of the river. How did that feel? I am sure you felt comfort and relief—and that is great. But what does it prove? This exercise goes to show you that everything you want is in the direction of the current of the stream; downstream, not upstream. If, for some reason, you were not feeling well before you started the exercise, you must realize it was because of your resistance to the natural flow of the river. Each time you go against the energy of Well-being, the result will be the same. Nevertheless, if you allow yourself to flow alongside, you will be amazed to see that things are progressing in the most natural, easy and unconstrained way.

You are probably wondering why this is happening. The explanation is quite simple. Given that you are an integral part of the universe, you are also made up of the same energy—the energy of Well-being; at the core of your existence. Accordingly, it stands to reason, that you feel best when you are aligned and coordinated with that energy.

It is extremely important to know that experiencing the energy of Well-being—leading a life of happiness and health—is nothing but your natural condition.

1 by Jerry & Esther Hicks, from the book "Ask and it is given", 2010, "http://www.AbrahamHicks.com

You must also realize that the energy of Well-being is constantly flowing: either towards you or from you; but it will not manifest, unless you allow it.

If you want to get the most out of the application of the Law of Deliberate Creation, you must recognize that truth. As I mentioned before, the first step is to be aware of where the focus of your thoughts lies. If your thoughts are in accord with the energy of Well-being—the energy derived from the core of your existence—you will feel fine. If not, you will feel discontent. This is how you can tell whether you are aligned with the realization of your goal or, instead, with the possibility of failure.

The following is an example of how this analogy (of the boat and the current) applies to our daily lives: Imagine that you are at work and your boss tells you that two days from now you have to go on a business trip. At first, you feel displeased because you may have planned something else, you may have many chores to do around the house, or just because you feel tired already. Your discomfort is proof that you are rowing upstream—against the current of Well-being. If, on the other hand, you just accept the fact, let go of your negativity and focus your attention on the positive things that this journey may bring (i.e. the opportunity to show your skills in a different environment, learn something new, meet new people, see new places, taste new flavors, or simply take a break), then you are heading downstream. Having embraced the energy of Well-being, you now feel peaceful and balanced; and this experience will add on to the experiences that help you reach your overall goal: professional growth, or simply an improved quality of life.

OBTAINING THE VIBRATION OF THE OBJECT OF YOUR FOCUS

Now we move on to something different. As I said before, when you give your undivided attention to a situation or object, you must keep in mind that the latter already pulsates with some kind of vibrating energy. As you maintain focus, you begin to pulsate with the same vibration. In other words, every time you focus on something, in a consistent and persistent manner, your energy becomes aligned with the energy of what you are thinking.

Here is an example: Upon receiving a utility bill, you realize that you do not have the money to pay for it. This situation will probably generate feelings of confusion, insecurity, or even fear. The more you hold on to those thoughts, the more your feelings intensify. According to the Law of Attraction, emotions are energy and, as such, they attract other, similar thoughts or situations. Basically, you are letting yourself become part of a vicious cycle—constantly recycling the things you do not want.

We talked earlier about convictions. At this point, I will supply a slightly different definition (a more energy-related one), about how convictions are formed and how they weigh on our actions.

It is true, that every time you focus on something and tune into its vibration, the alignment process itself becomes easier and more automatic, until you manage to attain the resonance of the thought, object, or situation to which you give your attention. Once you obtain the pulsating frequency, alignment will take place within seconds. Apparently, the more you focus on a thought, the more you get used to its vibration and the effect it has on you; creating what we call a conviction.

Accordingly, conviction is a thought—that you have heard or made many times in the past— which is charged with accumulated energy. The thought seems more real, with every single repetition and with every intense emotion it generates. Somewhere along the line, the repetitive thought—the belief— turns into a conviction and is now activated automatically, guiding your actions without you realizing it.

Let us look again at the previous example. You are in a situation where you do not have enough money to pay your bills and that creates fear, anxiety and doubt. The Law of Attraction responds to the negative vibration, resulting from the thought "I have no money", by bringing you more situations of shortage or debt, thus feeding the cycle of non-deliberate creation. In case these thoughts last for a long time, every time you receive a utility bill, you will have an automatic reaction of discomfort. And this reaction is unlikely to change, even when you are no longer in financial distress.

To sum up, a conviction is a vibration that you have practiced time and again. In other words, if you practice enough on a thought, it turns into a conviction. Every time you come across something that relates to that belief, you automatically pulsate with its vibration. It will not be long before the Law of Attraction recognizes that conviction, and its energy as your natural point of attraction, and starts bringing you situations that match that vibration. Similarly, as you gain more life experiences that are compatible with those beliefs, you will arrive at the conclusion that every conviction you have is true; since your own life attests to their reality, every single time!

Anything that attracts your attention becomes your truth. Your life and the lives of others are nothing but reflections of your dominant thoughts and convictions. Without doubt or exceptions, your inner reality is the creator of your outer reality.

THE CREATIVE PROCESS

The creative process is quite simple. It consists of three steps:

| STEP 1 | Ask for the things you desire with precision and clarity |

The first step is easy, so it usually comes naturally. Our conscious or subconscious desires derive from our everyday experiences. They are the byproduct of our exposure to an environment of extraordinary variety and contrast. Every time we see an object or experience a situation, our brain begins processing whether it is to our liking or not. Through this process, our brain forms desires and reaches decisions. What should we look out for in this process? We should always express what it is we want, not what we do not want. It seems that most of us are very clear about what we do not want, but are usually not able to figure out and voice our true desires.

In order to successfully play the game of deliberate creation, it is important to understand that although your requests are sometimes expressed through your words, most of the time, they emerge from the vibration that your body emits: through the emotions created by your thoughts.

Examine the following example: You see a homeless person on the street. You immediately assess your own situation and decide, there and then, to provide yourself with abundance and comfort. The sight of the homeless person, in this case, works as a stimulus encouraging you to consciously pursue prosperity. In case the sight of the homeless person evokes, instead, negative thoughts of fear and repugnance, it is apparent that—as your vibration sends this message to the universe—you are bound to receive situations that are consistent with fear and disgust. That could mean a lot of things, i.e. that everywhere you look you now see homeless people, constantly read articles about them, or even hear about someone you know who recently lost his home.

If you had no previous knowledge of the laws, this kind of experience might as well have been yours. Now you can try another strategy: once you see something you dislike or something that fills you with negative emotions (as in the previous example), acknowledge the experience as someone else's, think of the different life choices you make and declare that positive intent. As soon as you do this, your thoughts and, therefore, your vibration will detach from the unpleasant and will, in turn, align with the positive element you wish to experience.

|STEP 2 | The universe will provide the answer |

This next step is easy, as you are not required to do anything at all. It is up to the universe, the source of infinite energy, the energy of Well-being, or whatever else you like to call it.

As we have already said, although your requests are often expressed with words, most of the time, they surface automatically and unconsciously, through the vibration generated by your thoughts and feelings. And with no exception, all your demands are answered; every single prayer and all the things you have ever wanted are now handed to you.

However, if you still feel that you have yet to experience many personal desires, this is because you are not aware of all the laws, and as a result you fail to allow yourself to receive that gift.

|STEP 3 |Allow yourself to receive your request |

You have to allow yourself to receive the things you desire. In case you are not there yet—in a state of reception—you may be under the impression that your requests remain unanswered, even if that is not true. The third step is about the process where you match the vibration frequency of your thoughts and emotions with the vibration frequency of your desires. Same way you tune into the radio to receive the signal of the station you want to listen to.

In that light, you can realize that you are the ultimate creator of your life. From the apparent nothing, you can create anything you want, provided you give it your undivided attention, consciously and consistently.

Keep in mind that the only condition for creation is to be aligned with what you want to experience. Your thoughts, your vision, your expectations, your intentions, your beliefs, your emotions, your behavior, your words, your actions and your achievements must all be aligned with what you want to create.

Truth be told, there are plenty of distractions. In this technological age that we live in—where we have direct access to almost anything that goes on in our immediate environment or even our distant planet—we are constantly bombarded with thoughts and ideas that occasionally invade our personal experiences. And because of the existence of those distractions (that plethora of ideas and thoughts that we receive from our external environment), it is almost impossible to reckon that we can control our thoughts. The paradox here is that you think that paying attention to what is right in front of you makes total sense; whereas that is exactly the thing that sets you off course; as it hardly ever concerns you or your pursuits.

Precisely for that reason, I do not advise you to try to control your thoughts. I am, though, urging you to direct them. Given that the Law of Attraction magnetically attracts and reveals your thoughts in the physical dimension, were you to knowingly guide those thoughts, you would have a powerful weapon in hand that would provide you with an advantage in pursuing your goals.

THE EMOTIONAL POINT OF REFERENCE

Let us now consider the way in which you can direct your thoughts and how that shapes the emotional reference point which dictates action and creation.

As I mentioned before, whenever you concentrate on a particular thought, that is the exact moment when its vibration activates; and the Law of Attraction sends you an immediate response. The response could be in the form of new congruent thoughts that reinforce, intensify and embellish your original thought.

As you maintain focus on the same topic, your thoughts continue to enlarge and expand. Each new thought is more powerful than those that preceded it and produces a new one that is even stronger, and so on.

By now you know that the object of your focus already carries with it some vibration energy. So long that you maintain your concentration, you too will begin to pulsate with the same energy. Consequently, every time you focus on the same situation and every time you emit the same vibration, the vibration-identification process becomes easier and more familiar. In time, you will obtain a pulse frequency of your own. The result of the process is that, either in the short-run or in the long-run (depending on your degree of familiarization), you will be in a position to transform you current energy, as well as adopt a new one.

Basically, your constant focus—on an idea, thought, or situation—has prompted you to develop an emotional predisposition and thus an automatic behavior. That emotional predisposition is your reference point and guides you through life.

To illustrate, let us look at the following two examples:

- Think of a child whose family had always faced some kind of economic hardship. The child's parents would always talk about their lack of money and their inability to buy the things they needed or wanted. At home, the discussion would always revolve around feelings of sadness, frustration and fear. Even more so, expressions of the type, "money doesn't grow on trees" and "just because you want it doesn't mean you get it" would often be heard around the house. It is very likely that due to the child's long-term exposure to these thoughts and behaviors, his disposition on money issues—his emotional reference point regarding the prospect of economic success—would be quite poor. This would also mean that every time he would think of either money or abundance, he would immediately start to feel frustrated, sad, or deprived.

- Also, imagine a boy who witnessed, first hand, the death of his best friend's mother in a car accident. Given that the two children had a very intimate relationship, the heavy emotional trauma suffered by the girl, somehow, stirred up a very unsettling feeling in the boy: a constant fear for the wellbeing of his own parents. As a result, every time the boy's parents would take their car to drive somewhere, he would be terrified. Gradually, the fear developed into a habit; worrying about his loved ones. Insecurity, therefore, became his emotional reference point regarding the people he loved.

You must come to understand that reference points, vibrations, are developed with regard to every situation you encounter and every aspect of your life. You may, for instance, have a high reference point in the professional area and thus enjoy a great career, but at the same time have a low reference point in the area of social relationships. Or you may have a wonderful and trusting family, but not be successful in finding reliable business partners.

Why is it, then, that identifying your emotional reference point (pertaining in particular to the significant matters of your life), is of such great importance? On account that, it reflects and denotes your vibration in view of each and every situation that is presented to you. Actually, this is the vibration that the

Law of Attraction responds to—the life experience that you recycle. If the experience is positive, you have done well. If however it is negative, then you might want to intervene, knowingly and deliberately, to change it.

CONSCIOUSLY CREATING A NEW DOMINANT THOUGHT

By now, you should realize that the focus of your attention inevitably becomes your truth. Your life and the lives of others are nothing more than a reflection of the emotional reference point that derives from your dominant thoughts—no exceptions made.

It is, therefore, in your best interest to focus consistently on a matter that interests you and, with the use of perseverance and discipline, allow your desire to become the dominant thought. In turn, this activated thought will generate a corresponding positive vibration; intensified with every repetition. Accordingly, your emotional reference point will be formed, enabling you to attract your desires.

And this is a law.

The following example goes to show you the practical application of the law. A woman, former senior executive, suddenly lost her job and was unable to find employment elsewhere. Twenty months later, at the time I started working with her, her mind was still in a state of confusion and she could not clearly express the kind of employment she would actually like to attract. Her thoughts were constantly centered on the lack of work and what that meant for her. She was so ashamed of being unemployed that she basically took all the blame for it; saying that her condition was only the result of her incapability. She believed that she would have to settle for less than what she desired, but that was a thought she could not bear. Needless to say, it was because of that thought that she had failed in all her previous attempts to find work. To make matters worse, she was feeling a great deal of stress about her financial predicament. All in all, the situation was critical. And, of course, her emotional point of reference—her vibration—was filled with discomfort, disappointment and low self-esteem.

As is the case with most people, her basic problem was that she had a permanent focus on what she did not want; without even realizing it. Therefore, she constantly recycled negative thoughts that weakened her and worn her out.

Where she to get out of this situation, her first step would be to make a list of all the business goals she had accomplished to this day. So she began writing them down—reluctantly at first—but the more she wrote, the more she seemed to concentrate on positive thoughts. Each new thought led to another, also positive, and it was not long before her energy began to rise and a feeling of worthiness came over her. By the end of the process, she had written down thirty seven examples of professional success.

More than ever before, she was then able to shape and adopt a new, conscious, and empowering dominant thought: "I am now in a position to succeed in all of my pursuits." Building on that thought, and driven by its resulting emotions and energy, she finally managed to form and articulate a new professional goal, in a way that filled her with enthusiasm and anticipation. Having that as her new emotional point of reference, it only took my client forty five days to find the employment opportunity she wanted.

It is important to understand that only when you deliberately direct your thoughts, can you deliberately influence your point of attraction.

You cannot keep on thinking, believing, feeling, and talking about the things that trouble you in the way you did in the past, for it will not bring you the desired result. It will neither change your experiences, nor change your vibration and your point of attraction. Just like, you cannot listen to your favorite radio station, when you are tuned into another frequency.

Your thoughts, your emotions, and consequently your vibration frequencies must be in accord with your desires.

EMOTIONS: YOUR GUIDANCE SYSTEM

Now is the time to examine the role of emotions in our lives, as well as their contribution to the creation of our desires.

In all likelihood, most of you have never paid too much attention to your feelings. You probably have rarely pondered over the role they play in your lives, or you have simply failed to understand that role. There are times when they weigh you down, and there are times when they make you ecstatic. And all along, you reduce them to uncontrolled emotional reactions to everything that happens around you.

But, that is not the case. The role of emotions is extraordinary and anything but random! Every emotion conveys a specific message: whether and to what extent you are aligned with the energy of your inner self—at the core of which lies the energy of Well-being. Therefore, your emotions are indicators of the vibration divergence between what you are experiencing and who you actually are: your true self. In a way, it is an internal compass that helps you move forward on the path of your desires. If you do not learn how to properly use it, you remain vulnerable to any psychological or emotional storm that may hit your path.

Basically, emotions can be used as a guidance system to understand your vibrations and thus your point of attraction 1.

Every emotion carries a different frequency and vibration. The negative or less productive emotions have a low frequency vibration. Similarly, the positive or more productive ones have a high frequency vibration. Your goal is to make the transition from emotions of low vibration to emotions of high vibration, as depicted in the diagram below. As you begin to climb up the emotional steps, you improve your vibration and further align yourself with the energy of Well-being. Obviously, that is very important because the more your alignment improves, the more you will be able to create the experiences you want.

1 Jerry & Esther Hicks, from the book "Ask and it is given", 2010, HYPERLINK "http://www.AbrahamHicks.com/" \h   www.AbrahamHicks.com,

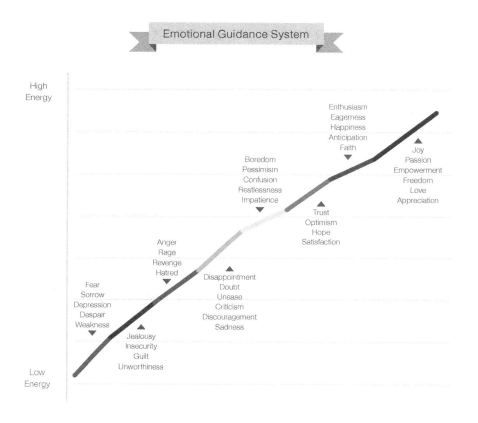

MAKING THE TRANSITION TO EMOTIONS OF HIGHER LEVEL

In order to benefit from the use of the Emotional Guidance System, you must first understand the message it conveys. Your emotions indicate whether your dominant thoughts are powerful or, instead, inhibiting. If you feel happy, hopeful and motivated, there is no concern. You are clearly on the right track and your thoughts are in alignment with your natural condition: the energy of Well-being. But when you feel nervous, angry or desperate, immediate action must be taken to help align your energy.

To make that happen, you must do the following:

- Look for the conscious thought or conviction that inferred that negative feeling. Usually, this is not an easy task because convictions are

53

deeply rooted in the way we think, and are often mistaken for being true. That goes to show you, that you are not always in a position to acknowledge the fact that they restrict you. You will have to show patience and perseverance, so as to give yourself enough time to get the answers you seek. When you finally locate those restricting beliefs, write them down on a piece of paper. It is preferable to refrain from judging or analyzing them; simply let them flow and record them.

○—¤ As soon as your conscious mind reveals your limiting beliefs, go ahead and doubt them! Ask yourself whether these are true or you have rather inherited them from your surroundings. While concentrating on them, try to understand how they make you feel; do they empower you or do they weaken you and lower your self-esteem?

○—¤ The final step of the process requires that you embrace a new, empowering dominant thought and constantly repeat it to yourself. Though you may not think so at first, repetition will in fact fill you with positive energy, and before you realize it, you will have taken a step up the emotional ladder—a step up on your system of emotional guidance.

○—¤ From this new position, you will be able to attract even more empowering and productive thoughts which will offer you a better vibration and more productive emotions. Through this consistent and step-by-step process, you will advance to the upper parts of the scale, until such moment where you find your natural state: the state of Well-being.

If you are wondering what kind of thoughts you can make, to generate positive and beneficial emotions (step 3 of the above process), the answer is simple: purposefully focus on what you want to experience.

It holds true, that most of us have a hard time distinguishing between the thought that reflects the things we want and the thought that reflects their lack of—mainly because we were not trained to think in this way.

It seems a lot simpler, though, to recognize the emotional impact produced by our thoughts, either on the desire itself, or on the absence of desire. In the first case we feel good, whereas in the second we feel bad.

In fact, when you are completely concentrated on your desire, you feel wonderful and your vibration reflects so. Conversely, when you focus on the absence or lack of what you really want, your get a feeling of discomfort that also reflects that emotion. In essence, your emotions will always reveal your vibration and your point of attraction. Only by paying attention to your emotions and making deliberate thoughts (which affect the way you feel), can you consciously direct yourself to the vibration frequency that will allow you to walk down your chosen path.

In light of that, I strongly advise you to use your emotional guidance system to strategically implement the Law of Deliberate Creation.

IN WHAT WAY AND HOW FAST CAN YOU MOVE UPWARDS?

The how and when of moving on to higher emotional scales usually depend on several factors: the severity of your situation, the intensity of your emotions and the length of time that you have been having them.

In the event that your situation is chronic or especially painful, maybe you should begin with taking baby steps. Often it is easier to convert, i.e. sorrow to disappointment than to attempt going from sorrow to happiness all at once. And that is legitimate because, even so, you are still making progress with your energy emission; in the sense that disappointment has a higher vibration than sorrow. Likewise, you may then make the transition from disappointment to restlessness, from restlessness to optimism, and so. In this light, your path becomes easier, more realistic and thus more productive.

YOU CAN CONTROL THE THINGS YOU BELIEVE

Most people do not know that they can have control over the things they believe in. Accordingly, they waste their lives observing the facts, without realizing that they have the ability to control their personal rapport with them. As a new thought gains ground, your emotional understanding tells you whether this thought of higher vibration is compatible with the energy of your inner self.

- If it is, your positive emotions will reveal it

- If it is not, your negative emotions will also reveal it

Provided you focus on your present reality and give out a positive or negative vibration, the Law of Attraction will respond by sending you a similar transmission. Let us assume that you are facing financial difficulties. As you contemplate on that reality, fearing that you do not have enough money to cover your household expenses—feeling anxious and insecure—you unintentionally offer a negative vibration. The law responds to the negative vibration of shortage, by bringing you more of such experiences; feeding the cycle of non-deliberate creation.

Even if it is not obvious, you are basically creating your values and beliefs system—a system that operates automatically—based on what your program stipulates. But only if you remove yourself from the cycle, begin focusing on the things you want out of life, and offer a positive, harmonious vibration, will you have applied the Law of Deliberate Creation.

As a rule, when the active thought is generic and not very focused, its energy level is low and so it lacks in attraction power. It is therefore possible that, in these initial stages, you will not get to enjoy the whole experience, only the basic parts.

Though you may not be able to prove it, the attraction of other, similar, congruent thoughts continues to exist. In short, the thought becomes empowered, while its force of attraction is increased and gives rise to other thoughts of similar attraction. And you now begin to realize how emotionally compatible is this advanced, vibration-wise, thought with the energy of your source. Whether it matches your inner self, your positive emotions will attest to that, and vice versa.

If, for instance, during your childhood years, you often had people tell you: "you are an incredible kid", "you will lead a fulfilling and happy life", "you have been blessed with so many talents" and "the world will be a better place because of you", there is no doubt that you felt good, as those messages were aligned with the essence of your existence.

If, on the contrary, as a child you were on the receiving end of messages such as: "you are a bad kid", "you must be ashamed of yourself", "I can't stand you" and "you are a lazy, useless brat", in all probability you felt bad, because those words would subconsciously divert your vibration from who you really are and what you really know of yourself.

In short, the way you feel is an accurate indication of the degree of your alignment with your inner self. To that effect, you can look to your emotions to discover whether you allow or obstruct the connection with your inner self.

As soon as you accept that for someone to have any kind of experience he must give his undivided attention to it, you will come to understand that every truth exists on exactly the same premise. Take, for instance, the economic crisis in Greece. Clearly, if anyone focus on the crisis—since most of the people around him are doing exactly that—he will most probably be headed for hard times. Nevertheless, were he to look outside his narrow span, he would realize that not everyone is affected by the crisis. There are those who were able to focus on something else and are now enjoying a life of abundance and growth. Not because they were lucky, but because they applied—either consciously or subconsciously—the process of deliberate creation. In any case, it is all about the things that you convert to truth: things that can be both wonderful and unpleasant. Deliberate creation relates to the purposeful selection of experiences that you convert to truths.

Through purposeful evaluation of your feelings, you will become even more efficient in directing your energy to where you want it to go and not the other way around. With practice, you will be able to control the focus of your creative energy, and much like an experienced sculptor, you will be overjoyed when it takes shape and form— your own creative project. If you want to become a disciplined, deliberate and happy creator, you need to practice.

Dominant Thought
• Deliberate focus for a time period

Conviction
• Long-term dominant thought
• Point of attraction

Your truth

THE MEANING OF ENERGY INTENSITY AND ENERGY VELOCITY

When you focus your energy on a specific experience, you must consider the intensity and the velocity of the energy you transmit. You also have to take into account the degree to which you accept or obstruct, even unwillingly, the creation of that experience.

Basically, these energy variations are consistent with two things: the time you have invested in contemplating your desire and whether you are explicit and firm in your request. When you have spent time on a desire, you clearly have a stronger appeal than as with a momentary thought.

Right now, can you think of something that you want? Something that you believe will come true? No doubt, you feel eagerness and sweet anticipation. Is it possible that you instead ponder upon something you still have not received? Might it be that you are focused on that thought? To this effect, you must be overcome with strong, negative feelings. Because sustained thoughts result in too much accumulated energy that cannot possibly be aligned with your vibration.

From the way you feel at this exact moment, you can tell whether you are aligned with your desire or, conversely, with the absence of your desire. That is, whether you are in a state of permission or obstruction.

APPLYING THE LAW OF DELIBERATE CREATION

Deliberate creation is quite satisfactory. You must knowingly focus on your thoughts and acknowledge the responses you receive in exchange for that. In this way, you will be able to guide your life to even more pleasant outcomes. It is indeed very agreeable being able to change your current situation, i.e. from sickness to health, from shortage to abundance, from dysfunctional relationships to harmonious ones.

I hope by now you have understood that deliberate creation regards your personal connection with you inner self; a connection that leads you to creation. Even though creation itself—the awareness of the things we desire:

objects, situations or events—is important, it is the process and the journey that define our experience.

For example, it is remarkable to own—via attraction—a new, lovely house, but bear in mind that the essence of life is in the process of attaining that goal. At first, you feel slightly unsatisfied with your present home. You then make a smooth and pleasant transition to the second phase, where you sort out your personal preferences. At the same time, you align your vibration with the notion and the details of your ideal house. Last step in the process is to monitor and consciously handle situations and events, until you finally accomplish your goal.

We can, therefore, conclude that in order to create what you want you have to select your dominant thought and deliberately focus on it for a period of time. The long-term and consistent focus on a dominant thought turns it into a conviction. That conviction will constitute your truth, as well as your emotional point of reference (your attraction point) from now on. It will also determine the energy you will be able to transmit, hereinafter, into the universe. To that effect, you may engage your emotional guidance system that will help you stay on track and move you closer to the desired result, one step at a time.

Every time you are successful in producing a certain outcome, in reality, you create. In essence, deliberate creation is all about attaining the result you want. The conscious management and maintenance of your vibration balance, over time, is what it takes for you to experience the deliberate Well-being.

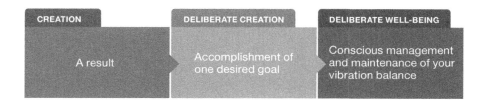

When assuming the role of Deliberate Creator, it is imperative that you understand the significance of purposeful intention, as well as the value of setting goals and focusing on the results you want. Nonetheless, the outcome depends mostly on how efficiently you manage your energy balance and the way that you align yourself with the object of your desire.

Going forward, as you better understand and apply the processes presented herein, you will enjoy every step of the journey of creation, even before you receive the things that you desire. Your life experience will be a constant source of joy, instead of occasional moments of satisfaction.

Chapter 3
THE LAW OF "ALLOWING"

To recognize our personal value and
the value of others, and to liberate
from inhibiting thoughts and
convictions, allows for the presence
of desires in our experiences.

DEFINITION OF THE LAW OF "ALLOWING"

Up to this point, you have learned that the most powerful law in the universe is the Law of Attraction which is based on the premise: "What resembles self will attract self." Also, there is the Law of Deliberate Creation which states: "I attract the object of my thought. With emotion and consistence, I attract the object of my thought even faster."

You have probably noticed that, in real life, whenever something bad happens, it is usually reinforced with added hardships. As a result, you are led to believe that everything is off-track. If you start your day with negative thoughts, you will probably have a difficult day ahead. If, on the other hand, you start your day feeling positive, the odds are in your favor. Actually, thoughts attract one another and gain in power the more time you invest in them. That which manifests is the direct reflection of what you are thinking and feeling.

If you succeed in comprehending and applying these two laws, you will have significantly improved your knowledge on how the universe functions and thus how things work in your life. Namely, you will have accepted and realized the fact that you are the creators of your own experiences and, as such, you can consciously choose the life experience of your desire.

For any of that to come true, you must first ensure that you have taken into account the Law of "Allowing".

The Law of "Allowing" refers to the principle of non-resistance. When you adopt a behavioral pattern of resistance towards people and situations, you deprive yourself of the possibility to be effective in creating the things you desire. In short, you get in the way of the creative process. If, however, you refrain from resisting, but choose to allow, then you are entitled to total freedom for action.

To illustrate this, let us examine the analogy below: Think of a fully-equipped kitchen, containing a wide variety of materials—all at your disposal. It is up to you to decide what recipe you want to make and which materials to use. Now, imagine that the materials in the kitchen are your life experiences. Though every experience is available to you, you are only interested in the ones that you like to bring into your life. At the same time, the others are of no interest to you, but they do not bother you either.

Let us assume that you want to make a cake (the objective). You know what ingredients you need and how to combine them (the strategy), in order to make the cake you want. As you go forward with the recipe (the creation process), there are still many ingredients lying around that are not suitable for this recipe, yet you do not worry or fuss over them. You understand that some of them are in harmony with your creation, while others are not. However, you do not feel the need to remove them all from your kitchen, because clearly they cannot be added to your cake—cannot be part of your creation—unless you put them there yourself. As long as you are clear about what ingredients are in sync with your creation, you have no concern for the wide variety of ingredients available. You therefore permit the existence of all materials and concentrate only on the ones you want to add to your creation.

The message of the Law of "Allowing" is simple: focus on the things that interest you and allow all others to just be. In effect, the Law of "Allowing" refers to the principles of acceptance of one's self and others, and non-resistance in the creative process.

Must like the other laws that govern the universe, the Law of "Allowing" is eternal, universal and absolute. It exists regardless of your acceptance. Knowingly or not, it affects your life. And this is something you need to understand and consciously apply.

> The Law of "Allowing" refers to the principles of acceptance of one's self and others and of non-resistance in the creative process

THE LAW OF "ALLOWING" IN THE CREATIVE PROCESS

In the previous chapter, we discussed the three steps that you must take in order to create anything that you desire:

- Step 1: Ask for what you desire with precision and clarity

- Step 2: The universe will respond to your request

- Step 3: Allow yourself to receive the answer

In this chapter, we will cover the third step that basically refers to the practical application of the Law of "Allowing".

In essence, this law is about relinquishing our need to control situations or people in our lives and accepting them as they are.

Indeed, control—although one of the most known action strategies—can have a serious and adverse effect on creation. For the simple reason that it obstructs the flow of Well-being, which always comes our way, and hinders our efforts. If, for instance, you want to water your garden, but you keep the water valve turned off, the flow is obstructed and water cannot go through. Yet, it is not lack of water which causes the problem. It is rather the valve—the control—that obstructs the flow of Well-being and renders you incapable of receiving the things that life has to offer.

Whether you were to let yourself believe in the creative process and allow situations to evolve, you would be more suited to receive your desires. Instead of holding yourself responsible for every little detail, you may choose to show faith to the Laws of the Universe and allow for things to happen.

Indisputably, when you try to control everything, you lose sight of the bigger picture. You are looking at the tree, rather than the forest. You tend to forget that there is a universal intelligence, greater than your own, that can better orchestrate the evolution of events: from the little, ordinary things all the way to your grandest expectations.

If you are in doubt of either the existence or the purpose of this higher intelligence, all you have to do is to observe the physical world to discover infinite examples of exactly that. To quote Deepak Chopra: "grass doesn't try to grow, it just grows, birds don't try to fly, they just fly, the sun doesn't try to shine, it just shines, the baby doesn't try to be happy, it just is, the Earth doesn't try to rotate, it just does and it is the nature of man to realize his dreams, easily and effortlessly."

In effect, your shift in perception can and will activate the Law of "Allowing". As long as you adhere to a frame of thought that entails faith, as well as disengagement from the need for control, you will be all set to receive everything that you have asked for. The more you relinquish your need to control things, the more you allow abundance, happiness and success to flow inside your life.

Let us examine things on a deeper level. This particular law consists of two parts:

- Allow yourself and others to be who they are

- Allow the universe to deliver to you everything you want and allow yourself to receive it

ALLOW YOURSELF AND OTHERS TO BE AS THEY ARE

If you can allow yourself to be the real you; that is to say part of the universe, then the Law of "Allowing" will unfold right in front of your eyes. When you are motivated by the energy of love and acceptance, you are in fact applying the principle of non-resistance and your positive energy is flowing. Accordingly, inspiration and creativity emerge from within and you are in a better position to move forward with the creation of what you desire.

If, on the contrary, you believe that someone else has to think, to feel, or to act on the basis of what you think he should, you are definitely out of sync with the law. In short, you seem to hold on to certain perfect thoughts that can bring a great deal of pain into your life and your relationships. More specifically, that behavior is the exact opposite of accepting others the way they are. Let us look more closely at the first part of the law.

You to be who you are Others to be as they are	The Law of "Allowing"

It is possible that your need to control things and enforce them on others, masks a feeling of fear and doubt regarding yourself. Maybe, that is your way to affirm your personal value.

For example, if you dislike obese people, make fun of them or reject them, because you consider them either weak or sick, that could be your way to affirm that you are better, stronger, or even healthier. Even if you show signs of addiction yourself; given that you are, for example, a heavy smoker, a workaholic, or a compulsive gossiper. When you belittle others and question their value, the case may be that it is all part of your strategy to feel better about yourself; even if you do so unknowingly.

Conversely, the fear of not measuring up to the perfect images which you are holding in mind—in spite of your constant efforts—makes you vulnerable.

Because, if others go about it differently, what does that mean for you? Are you the one who is wrong?

To judge and criticize others does not absolve you of your responsibility. In the example of the obese man where you fail to apply the Law of "Allowing", it is likely that you will want to avoid him or detest him even. Perhaps, on a subconscious level, it is because you want to make sure that there is no such threat in store for you; to eliminate all possibility of ever becoming weak in character. However, the more energy you put into such negative thoughts or words, the more you invite this kind of experiences into your life.

Under the Law of Attraction, the more we judge people, the more we attract people who judge us. If instead you accept—and not just tolerate—diversity, then you have understood the Law of "Allowing". In point of fact, tolerance shows resistance and rejection of others and their choices, even when not clearly expressed. On the other hand, acceptance shows love and understanding. Basically, these are two very different behaviors which emit dissimilar emotional vibrations and bring very different results in your relationships.

The Law of "Allowing" may be the most difficult to apply. Apparently, a lot of people have a hard time accepting it, in their hearts and minds, because it does not conform to common, daily behavioral patterns. One of the reasons is that criticism and gossip have infiltrated every social discussion and are widely regarded as acceptable behaviors. Unfortunately, given that not all people are aware of the Laws of the Universe, the negative side effects associated with those behaviors are not always detected. People are, therefore, reluctant to abandon them; hence the ongoing recycling of those negative results.

If you only feel good about yourself and your life, provided that everyone agrees with what you believe or want, you will never get to experience freedom. Judgment and criticism are the very opposites of freedom: they are obligation and imprisonment. Because you can never make the rest of the world behave in the way that you think they should. It is as if you are trying—in vain—to achieve the impossible.

Needless to say, that the opposite scenario cannot happen either: you cannot always act in a way that pleases other people. Especially, if that particular behavior is at odds with yourself or your real needs. The effort alone will cause you a great deal of pain and internal struggle, given that you deprive yourself of the right to be the person that you are.

To be in a position to apply the Law of "Allowing", you have to take a good look at yourself; accept, honor, respect, love and support who you are. Take the time to get to know yourself and make sure you have a clear picture of your needs, your values and beliefs. Identify the rules that govern your life and embrace your true identity. Furthermore, choose your values and beliefs system and release your talents and skills for the pursuit of infinite possibilities. Only when you have done that, will you become recipients; only then will you be able to honor, respect, love and support others.

For the purpose of efficiently applying the law, your thoughts and actions must be aligned with the law. With the knowledge you gain from this reading, you can begin your efforts right away. All you need to do is to adopt a new, deliberate, supportive thought: "I am who I am. Being me, I allow others to be who they are" and repeat it often.

Moreover, you need to accept the fact there are no two persons alike, even though they may share a lot of similar characteristics or beliefs. Everyone has a different life theory and believes in a different version of the world. Since everyone is different and unique, you have to allow others to do what they do and to have what they have. Refrain from judging them and try to be emotionally detached from their behaviors and actions.

There is a sense of freedom in allowing people and situations to be who and what they are; no matter what you feel about it. In fact, when you do not consent, you are in a state of resistance. And that resistance not only deprives you of your freedom, but also obstructs the free flow of Well-being. In any case, resistance is the opposite of "allowing".

Once again, I need to point out that in order to allow the things you want to flow in your direction, you have to allow others to focus on what they want, even when you disapprove.

PRACTICAL REALIZATION OF THE LAW OF "ALLOWING"

Once I got hold of the information pertaining to the Law of "Allowing", many of the situations in my life started making sense. It seemed that I had spent years judging others and comparing them to myself and my beliefs. Admittedly, passing judgment used to be one of my favorite pastimes. The thing is that, at the time, I was convinced that my model of the world was the right one, so whenever I met people whose behavior deviated from mine—particularly in matters of ethics, justice and respect of others—I felt great discontent.

A few years back, there was a man in my business environment whose beliefs regarding office organization and people management were diametrically different from mine. I used to observe the way he behaved and I would get upset. If that was not enough, I would talk about him for hours with my friends, after work. The situation deteriorated and soon there was this unspoken conflict between us. That was the time when I got hold of this information and since my previous thoughts and reactions had not been able to put an end to this vicious cycle of dispute, I decided to put to use the Law of "Allowing".

What I did was very simple.

On the same night, I took five minutes to really think about what would be the ideal business environment for me and the kind of relationship I would like to have with my colleagues. I embraced the idea that this man was doing the best he could, based on his own experiences and knowledge, and that he basically meant well. I, therefore, decided that the best I could do was to allow him to act in the way that his circumstances and knowledge permitted. I continued practicing on this exercise for a few more days.

Even today I am impressed by how remarkably well the Law of "Allowing" worked.

The result was astonishing! A week after I started applying the law, an important meeting came up that I feared would most likely lead to a dispute. Strangely enough, things went smoothly, and to top that, the man asked me to help him deal with a couple of human administration issues, as he felt he lacked the necessary experience.

To me, this is a clear depiction of how the Law of "Allowing" works in everyday life. While I was in a state of resistance, things were unpleasant. Yet, as soon as I abandoned my negative attitude and allowed that man to be all he could be, his behavior was no longer defensive. In that way, I managed to help myself, help him, and the entire department.

Since then, I apply this law on a daily basis, allowing people to be as they please. However, I am very clear about the role I am letting them play in my life. The application of the law has led me to enjoy a better, stronger and more essential relationship with my children, my family, my friends, and my business partners. The most amusing part, however, is to observe the law's amazing, constructive effect when we apply it in public places, for example: the tax office, the bank, even the supermarket.

Allow people to be who they are and act on the basis of their desires and abilities. If you find it difficult to conduct yourself in this manner, that—more or less—means you are unhappy with yourself and you project your discontent on others. In that case, take a look at yourself to realize what is happening, so that you choose an even better behavioral strategy next time. Allowing means:

- letting go of all judgment and emotional attachment regarding other people, their possessions and actions

- acknowledging other people's rights, same way you stand up for your own

- the essence of the words, "Love your neighbor with all his faults"

APPLYING THE LAW OF "ALLOWING" IN RELATIONSHIPS

Let us now look, in more detail, at how to use the Law of "Allowing" in your relationships.

In general, everyone understands, perceives and views life differently. Therefore, it is pointless to seek absolute agreement and consensus. Apparently, there are times that you will not be able to help yourself and will pass judgment on people and situations. But you have to realize that by judging, criticizing and opposing others, you are basically making it harder for yourself.

As we explained before, the phenomenon of action-reaction is present in this universe of attraction. The more you push against undesirable things, the more you will be in sync with that pressure, and the more you will receive pressure in the form of unwanted experiences. And as long as unwanted experiences keep coming your way, you will be affirming over and over the same convictions, thinking that you were right all along. In other words, the more you hang on to your convictions, the more the Law of Attraction will enable you to experience them, time and again.

On many occasions, socializing with others can be stressful or problematic. But asking them to be different is not the answer. Most people are not, in the least, interested in changing and—even if they wanted to—it is highly unlikely that they will be who you want them to be; because their inner self will react to the change.

When someone pushes your buttons and says or does something that bothers you, just tell yourself: "This man is neither good nor bad. He is neither a man I like, nor a man I dislike. He just is. He is one more person who does the best he can; according to his upbringing, his convictions, his situations, and his present needs and desires. Whatever he does is all about him—it has nothing to do with me."

It is equally important to realize that when someone pushes your buttons that alone implies that you have an unresolved issue. For the simple reason that, every comment and behavior you are currently receiving is what you previously sent out and now comes back to you. And you need to carefully analyze that fact, if you are to get to know yourself better.

Take this example: Supposedly, when you were a child, your parents were very demanding and nothing you ever did was ever good enough for them. Growing up, you always tried to please them or get their approval; but you never did. Consequently, you were led to believe that you are not good enough.

Now, you are an adult and you are an employee at a firm. You love your job and you try to do your best. At one point, you present your work to your supervisor and, while he seems generally pleased, your mind singles out—from the entire discussion—one little comment of his: where he asks you to make a minor correction. Although it is only a trivial matter—compared to the volume and quality of your work— it seems to have struck a chord, as you immediately begin to feel sad and disappointed.

The discomfort you are feeling is not because of your supervisor's comment, but because of what you believe about yourself. It dates back to your childhood conviction of not being good enough; rooted in your thoughts and in your vibration. Given that this vibration deviates from the energy of Well-being that flows through you, you feel sad and disappointed. If you wish never to feel that way again, changing your place of work or your department will certainly not suffice. What you could do, though, is to apply the process we learned in the previous chapter and change your vibration. The only vibrational alignment you need, in order to experience the things that you desire, is the alignment within you. It has nothing to do with anything or anyone else.

You must, therefore, understand that neither your supervisor nor other people around you are to blame for your reaction. And for that reason, you have to set them free and allow them to be themselves. In time, you will come to realize that each person you interact with brings you the amazing gift of knowledge, since he reflects your own energy vibration. Depending on the behaviors you receive or your reaction to them, you will be able to assert the degree to which you have applied the law and to further monitor your progress in higher levels of awareness and knowledge.

By now you know that in order to feel good you have to be aligned with the energy flowing at the core of your existence—the energy of Well-being. You also have to allow yourself to do what you think is right and free yourself from the behaviors of others.

At the same time, allow others to be, to have and to do as they wish; without trying to fix them, change them, or prove them wrong. That will get you nowhere; it will in no way bring you closer to your pursuits. Instead of trying to prove other people wrong for who they are or for what they do, simply assume the role of an observer and say: "That is something I choose not to accept and will not apply in my life. But I allow you to do the best you can."

You must realize that the only thing which can bring you closer to your desires is your own flow through life: your thoughts, beliefs and actions. Focus on yourself and on shaping the beliefs and actions that will lead you to progress, while at the same time allow for all other things to exist.

ALLOW THE UNIVERSE TO DELIVER YOUR DESIRES AND ALLOW YOURSELF TO RECEIVE THEM

Let us examine the second part of the law.

The Law of "Allowing"	The Universe to give you whatever you desire Yourself to receive it

When people get first acquainted with the Law of Attraction, they get excited about the possibilities, feel positive and eager to identify the object of their desire; expecting to bring enormous change to their lives. But when they cannot create what they want, they get confused. It is because they are unaware of the vibration that they transmit to the universe. In other words, you must acknowledge your present vibration and release all resistance or doubt. That you can accomplish by changing the inhibiting beliefs and the behaviors that created the resistance to begin with.

GAIN AWARENESS OF YOUR INHIBITING BELIEFS

In the previous section, we talked about inhibiting beliefs and how to get rid of them. Once again, I would like to urge you to locate and let go of all beliefs that restrict you.

The simple procedure of recognizing and questioning the validity of those inhibiting beliefs will make for a decisive step in your quest for change. Not only that, but you will also be able to derive great pleasure from the adoption of new and empowering beliefs.

RELEASE RESISTANCE

What is resistance? It is the negative emotions that keep you away from the flow of pure, positive energy.

Think of your body as a tube that is in direct connection with the energy of Well-being. When you feel absolutely positive and your energy is in a state of non-resistance, you are in direct flow and connection. Ideas, thoughts, inspiration, happy feelings and situations flow through you with ease. That happens naturally, much like your breathing. But when you are dealing with negative emotions (i.e. disapproval, depression, anger, fear, resentment, confusion, envy, jealousy, guilt, shame, frustration, doubt and boredom), it is as if you are using the water valve which obstructs the pipe and therefore prevents the pure and positive energy of the source to flow through you (as in our earlier example).

Whenever you are in the mood to creating something, but you hold negative feelings, those feelings get in the way of creation. They will always keep you away from what you desire. Only when you let go of resistance and return to a state of allowing will you be able to enjoy abundance, freedom, success, progress, wealth and joy.

As we explained in the previous chapter, your emotions are your allies in the pursuit of your goals. Since emotions constantly bring you messages concerning your alignment, or non-alignment for that matter, you can—at any time—decide to realign yourself and act differently. Nevertheless, it is your negative emotions that you have to pay particular attention to: the ones that cause you discomfort and the ones that literally encourage you to act in a way that re-positions you in the path of Well-being. We will now call these emotions: Action Signals. Given that we are usually unable to read these emotions and the message they bring, we get sucked in and we hold on to them for far too long.

When your mind is set on something that you have wanted for a long time and you feel bad for it has not yet happened, it is very likely that your feelings are both intense and unpleasant. If that thought persevered for a long time, it has possibly accumulated a lot of negative energy that not only prohibits your vibrational alignment, but perpetually recycles this unpleasant situation. The knowledge you gain herein will help you, at first, decipher the message you receive: the action signal. Next, you will have to look for a different interpretation of the situation; one that will give rise to emotions of higher vibration which will, in turn, help you choose another course of action.

The other day, one of my clients was telling me that, even though he begins his day by applying the method I have taught him, as the day unfolds those prior feelings of easiness and optimism gradually disappear. Because as soon as another employee, a co-worker, or a client steps into his office with a complaint of some sort, my client's positive disposition starts to fade.

I explained to him that this could be a one-of-a-kind opportunity for growth. It was obvious that whenever he joined in those discussions, he would begin relating to what the other persons felt. Admittedly, his discomfort was the result of their vibrations being very different from his initial vibration.

n other words, the discomfort he feels goes to show the deviation from his inner self, as he lets himself be carried away and becomes aligned with the events that take place in his external environment. It is not so much the subject of the discussion that causes his discomfort, but rather that he gradually distances himself—the more he gets emotionally attached to those discussions—from his previous positive disposition which was in sync with his inner self and the energy of Well-being. That was a great opportunity for him to grow, by deciphering the message—that is recognizing the action signal—and guiding himself to remain aligned with the energy of Well-being, inspite of what went on in his environment. It was a chance to break resistance and allow others to be, without getting emotionally attached.

YOUR VIBRATIONAL ALIGNMENT MUST ALWAYS COME FIRST

Let me expand on the boat analogy, from the previous chapter, by asking you, "Which way are you rowing?" It is very important to know the answer to this, for the following reason:

Not a single one of your desires is headed upstream!

When your inner vibration is out of sync with the infinite energy flow of the universe, the source, and your inner self, nothing you can do can solve the problem. There are no effective actions, words, thoughts or ideas deriving from a state of resistance or non-alignment. And to make matters worse, any attempt to take action will possibly lead to faulty decisions which will further aggravate things.

When you are experiencing a strong feeling of discomfort, the only thing you can do is to find a way to ease off emotionally and vibrationally. Only then, will you get right back on track, realigning your energy with more productive vibrations and actions. In your everyday lives, the relief—surrendering to the stream of the current—may come when you move away from what bothers you. In order to accomplish that, you can take a walk, go for a swim, play with your children, watch a comic show, sing or hum a favorite tune, dance, draw, etc. You may now choose the action that is more suited for you and apply it at times when you feel discomfort, and relieve yourself by letting go of the oars. It will mentally empower you and will help you become more efficient in handling that which bothers you. More specifically, there is a relevant procedure in the Workbook, to help you identify and apply ways to support yourself at times like these.

When you let yourself flow freely, in line with the current and without any resistance, alignment is expressed in the form of positive emotions. If you allow it to happen, the stream will guide you to the completion of all things you desire in your life.

Undoubtedly, your true power lies in the Law of "Allowing". The application of this law, along with the application of the other universal laws, will give you an unwavering advantage in shaping your action strategy.

THE MOST COMMON EXPRESSION OF RESISTANCE

We often strive to bring about the change we desire, believing that this change must take place immediately or as soon as possible. Yet, when we try to determine when and how the situation will improve, we are in fact standing in the way of improvement; because our ignorance (not knowing the answers) hinders our vibration. Accordingly, our impulse works against us.

When you feel the urgency of being somewhere else, you put pressure on the place you are at this exact moment. Indeed, your belief—that you must move on to a better place—questions the wisdom and the power of the current, its velocity, its direction, and its promise. It is as though you are rowing your boat upstream: away from what you desire.

The feelings you have at any given moment indicate two things:

- The speed of the river (the current), therefore the strength of your desire to attain whichever outcome.

- Your direction relatively to the current: upstream or downstream?

If your feelings are negative, you are probably focused on the absence of your desire and therefore you row upstream facing great resistance. If you are feeling positive, you are most likely focused on your desire and you are speeding downstream.

In case you belong to the first category, you must primarily seek relief. By doing so, you lessen your resistance. To reduce your resistance means that you flow in the direction of your desire. Accordingly, your desire will manifest itself to you, if it has not already.

Surely, with daily practice on guiding your thoughts downstream, that will, in time, become your natural tendency or predisposition. The process will increasingly become easier. At first, the feeling of relief may be temporary. Over time, however, the relief will be more permanent.

It is important to realize that, according to the Law of Attraction, the response to resistance is illness. Similarly, Well-being is the response to the successful application of the Law of "Allowing".

As per my earlier advice, when you begin working with the laws—in principle— try not to pressure yourself into making radical improvements or finding life- altering ideas right away. Aim initially at slightly improving the way you feel. Many situations may arise within a day. Attempt to comprehend how you feel in each and every one and try to gently steer them towards the flow of the river. Before you know it, this routine will have become your natural tendency and you will soon see your life changing.

WHAT IS CREATION?

What is the definition of creation? It is a mental process, not just an action process. It refers to the alignment of thoughts with a desired goal and is in no way limited by any action taken to accomplish that goal.

There is more to pursuing the things you want out of life than just action. It also involves the alignment of your thought's energy with the desired result. Moreover, it requires shifting your attention to the direction of your desire, instead of concerning yourself with whatever negative conditions triggered your desire to begin with.

And though, in the meantime, you may come up with some inspired action, when applying the laws you must aim for the alignment of the energy of your thought: a vibrational alignment.

What does that mean in real life? Take a look at the following examples:

When you realize that you weigh twenty five pounds more than you desire to, your first reaction should not be one of going on a strict diet or starting an intense workout to lose the extra weight. Your first reaction should be to clearly state your desire and the reasons behind it. To take a mental picture of yourself, as if you had already lost the extra pounds and returned to your normal weight. To envision all those exciting things that you will be able to do, once you get a much healthier and fit body.

When you realize that you are in need of more money, your first reaction should not be to resign from your current job and start searching for a new one. Your first reaction should be to abandon your feeling of deprivation and instead focus on the feeling of abundance, as the end result of your goal.

When you realize that you want to be appreciated in your work environment, your first reaction should not be one of direct contradiction with your supervisor, demanding that he respects you. Your first reaction should rather be to radiate self-respect, so that others follow your lead and respect you as well.

When you realize that you are unhappily married, your first reaction should not be to just walk out of your marriage. Your first reaction should be to turn to your inner self and try to look for a new and deeper understanding of who you are and what you are experiencing. Only in this way will you be able to interpret situations, assume your rightful role and assign new roles to those involved.

When you obtain vibrational alignment, any action seems inspired. Indeed, vibrational alignment yields outstanding results. On the contrary, without alignment, the outcome of your efforts can disappoint you or discourage you, as you draw the conclusion that what you desire is simply not there for you.

It therefore holds true that the Law of "Allowing" is the conscious, gentle guidance of your thoughts in the general direction of your desires.

At this point, I would like to comment again on how the works of the mind influence your action.

In the first example (the weight concern), choosing to have a dessert or not, has no effect whatsoever. The action alone is of no importance. That what matters most is your thought at the time you act and its energy vibration.

In that particular example, the gain of weight is not because of your action, it is the result of your vibration—your thoughts and feelings about what you are doing. So when you happen to have a craving for chocolate, if at that time you think it is something that you will enjoy and will make you happy, then—by all means—go ahead.

If, on the other hand, you think you shouldn't, but still cannot resist the temptation and eat it anyway, then the guilt or any similar emotion that you are having will make you "fat". That happens because your brain—now filled with negative thoughts and emotions—instructs your body to differently metabolize this food.

On occasion, you have probably met people who are extremely thin, although eating constantly. You may have even heard them brag about it, saying: "No matter how much I eat, I never gain weight!" Evidently, all they are doing is instructing their minds—right there and then—to work in a way that confirms this belief. Most likely, they have been doing so for years, knowingly or not. Let me assure you that this is the way things work in life: whatever you believe in and are in sync with, will manifest to you.

You need to take a little time to consider the ways in which you resist your desires. In the event that there is something missing from your life, this is undoubtedly your own doing—the result of your resistance.

The more you comprehend the presence of this powerful energy flow; as I am explaining it to you here, and start looking at the bigger picture of who you are, the more convinced you will be of the need to simply re-align yourself with the core of your existence. When you do that, the Law of "Allowing" will become your second nature.

I must point out that creation involves much more than making things happen through action. In essence, creation has nothing to do with making things happen. To create, in effect, means to allow things to happen via your vibrational alignment with them. And this might be a little difficult for you to accept at first. Most probably, your experience to date dictates that action brings results. And this is basically true. But to act, without first aligning your mind or your energy, can either be too difficult or too time-consuming.

The same holds true when you presume that action is the cornerstone of the creative process, but you fail to consider your own vibrational center. In that case, you operate at a disadvantage, because action alone is not powerful enough to off- set the competitive energy of your out-of-sync thoughts.

Contrarily, when the action you want is aligned with emotions such as: enthusiasm, motivation, joy, and anticipation, your vibration is harmonious. This means that you are eager to take action, and that this action will no less bring you positive results.

Consequently, if you begin by purposefully aligning your vibration, your vibration will then stimulate more successful action. Undoubtedly, this calls for a much more pleasant, more powerful and more efficient approach for anything you want to create.

WHY HAVE YOU NOT YET RECEIVED ALL THE THINGS YOU HAVE REQUESTED?

Imagine that everything you ever wanted and asked for, but still have not received, is kept in a magnetic energy bank. This bank safeguards your welfare, your health, your abundance and the Well-being you have created for yourself and have been providing for, ever since the day you were born.

Everything you have ever wanted out of life is there, waiting for you. But in order to get it, you must use the key that the laws of the universe entrusted you with.

All that is required from you to receive your request is to understand how the game is played and what your vibration tendencies are. Accordingly, you have to stop advertising the possible negative aspect of the experience that initially triggered your desire. Likewise, you must also be determined to move in the direction of the object of your desire.

Take this example: You are in financial trouble and all day long you think about your need for more money. Therefore, when you talk to yourself or others, you use expressions like, "I never have enough money" or "it is unfair that some have a lot and others have nothing at all". Based on what you have already learned here—with statements like these—you run the risk of actually depriving yourself of the emotional- energy vibration, necessary to obtain the money that you need.

That goes to show you that although your desires keep on piling up at your energy bank, you are still not able to receive them. And why is that? First of all, because your convictions to date never allowed you to believe that you could have anything you want. The second reason is that, before now, you did not have the key that would get you in. In short, you were unaware of the laws of the universe.

On the other hand, when you are in alignment with what you desire, you just go into this magic bank where everything has been taken care of, on your behalf. There are plenty of people who have already done so. Those who talk about what they want and not about what they do not want and who have learned to reward and not to judge. Those who are optimists rather than pessimists and who have trained themselves—one step at a time—to concentrate on their desires. With those behaviors, they have managed to improve their vibrational frequency that has, in turn, allowed them to step inside their energy bank and receive the things they want.

In any case, if you want the next one to receive the treasure to be you, you must identify your vibration with that; the key to the bank will open all doors for you!

APPLYING THE LAW OF "ALLOWING"

As I mentioned in the beginning of this chapter, the Law of "Allowing" basically refers to the release from the need to control situations or people in our lives and accepting them for what and who they are. It also talks about not resisting occurring events and surrendering to life's journey having faith. As we gain more clarity on how things work in the universe and we come to realize our true purpose, we can trust the laws to work to our benefit.

You can start today by adopting and applying the following, as means to a new life approach:

- Accept this moment as is, not as you think it should be.

- Realize how you feel and take responsibility for your emotions. Acknowledge the possibility to change the way you feel.

- Practice on being defenseless. When you try to defend your beliefs or convictions you are in the energy of resistance.

- Remember that energy is endless and only if you embark on this path without resistance, will you experience happiness and bliss and a life that flows effortlessly.

Chapter 4
THE LAW OF SUFFICIENCY AND ABUNDANCE

You are all part of the Universe.
The Universe is Infinite.
You are Abundance.

DEFINITION OF THE LAW OF SUFFICIENCY AND ABUNDANCE

We live in an abundant universe. We need only to look at nature to see that there is an unlimited display of remarkable things and experiences: the infinity of the stars, the foliage of trees and flowers, the waves, the pebbles and the sand; an immense collection of different animal and plant species. Not to mention, a diverse variety of human experiences, various types of happiness, successes and achievements. The Law of Sufficiency and Abundance works on the global premise that we are all born complete, sufficient and abundant. Given that the universe—the cornerstone of all creation— provides an infinite energy supply, there is a real possibility for all of us to excel in life.

Creative energy is also infinite and it is constantly reproduced in the natural world. It is everywhere, like an endless ocean of abundance. In other words, there is no limit to the amount of love, happiness, energy, and material abundance that we can create, enjoy, or experience.

How can we explain this? We already know that, in this world, we are all made of energy; everything is made of energy. That energy is in unlimited supply and is available to each and every one of us, at any point of time. Precisely to this, attests the fourth law of creation—the Law of Sufficiency and Abundance, which declares that:

> **Abundance is not only**
>
> **our birth right, it is what we are.**
>
> **We are abundance!**

It is very important to understand that when you were given the gift of life, you were also given access to the power you need to create the life you want.

Since the beginning of time, our enlightened leaders taught us that progress and prosperity are part of the natural process of life and that the lavish supply of abundance is intrinsic to all human beings. The secret is to gain awareness of this infallible principle and to understand that deficiency is simply the result of false beliefs. When you successfully modify those convictions, you too will be able to become part of this generous and constantly-expanding abundance.

Due to the infinite supply of goods, there is plenty to go around for everyone. With that in mind, if someone else happens to attain what you desire for yourself, you should not be worried. Instead, you should be excited at the prospect that soon you will get it as well. Life is not a pie cut in pieces where everyone wants to get the biggest slice. The actual meaning of the universe's infinity is that you too can get everything you want, without any limitations.

Why is it so important to be aligned with the Law of Abundance? For the reason that, things will become easier and will happen at a faster pace. Because you will be flowing alongside the energy current of Well-being—in a stream of happiness and positive creation—and from that position you can draw to your direction anything you desire.

Many of us feel that who we are, as well as what we have is just not enough. You now know that, when you abide by that thought, you will attract that which is not enough. Because, according to the law, your experience will confirm that insufficiency. So, if you feel that what you have falls short of your desires or thoughts, you will continue to experience situations of that kind.

It is important to understand the simple fact that there is no shortage of anything in the universe and that there is more than enough for all of us to meet our needs and desires.

Knowing the above, you must ask yourself: "When will I feel that I have enough? When will I feel satisfied?"

"When I lose twenty five pounds? When I have a million dollars in my bank account? When I find my ideal partner, when I land the perfect job, or when I get to own the house of my dreams?"

It appears that when you feel that you do not have enough, you are actually saying that you are not enough. However, if that is where you stand; regardless of what you do with your life, you will never feel complete. The reason is that beliefs, based on deprivation, affect your ability to create to a satisfying degree. Instead, they make you want what others have; in a constant struggle to compete and compare. Eventually, you will find yourself at a much weaker position to attract the things that you want.

ABUNDANCE AND DEPRIVATION: WHAT IS YOUR ORIENTATION?

This strong belief of deprivation and inadequacy that most of us share is rooted in the generations of the past: in the narrations of the war and the military occupation that our forefathers had gone through. From a very young age, we have been exposed to the horrible experiences of deprivation, during relevant discussions or through films and documentaries about the hardships of wars. It is therefore logical that a part of those indirect experiences has infiltrated our subconscious, mainly in the form of fear or aversion.

On the other hand, the establishments of modern society and economy—always encouraging the perpetual accumulation and consumption of goods—bombard us with messages which distract us from spiritual values and teach us that the experience of abundance or deprivation is associated with the acquisition of tangible goods or the lack thereof.

However, neither one of those two influencing factors—which have unfortunately determined most of our experiences and convictions—has anything to do with the truth that governs the universe. As a matter of fact, they are contrary to natural laws and remove us from the path of true fulfillment.

So, what is the difference between a man who embodies the Law of Sufficiency and Abundance and a man who is still found in a position of deprivation? Let us look at some examples:

The man who is in a state of deprivation and shortage basically struggles to meet life's demands, thinking he is always short of time or energy. The man who is instead grounded in abundance—in harmony with his natural dimension—is pleased and grateful for his full life and all the things he can accomplish throughout the day. The man who wants to improve his financial status through his work, but considers his life and himself as insufficient, is a man who constantly complains that others are being promoted while he is left behind. The man who sees his life and himself as sufficient, knows that he deserves to get ahead and, even if he does not get promoted, he remains motivated and focused; determined to maximize his worth and confident that a bigger opportunity will soon come along.

The man who wants to find a companion to form a meaningful relationship, but considers his life and himself as insufficient, is a man who always complains that the right person is nowhere to find. The man who sees his life and himself as abundant, feels that any outing or gathering is a fun and exciting opportunity to meet interesting people.

The man who considers his life and himself as insufficient, approaches life with the thought: "What will I gain from that?" Always questioning his value and the ability to produce the abundance he wants, he is unable to think beyond his immediate needs and the ways to meet them. He is in a mental trap which confines him in situations that are not what he desires. He is so concerned with what he can gain, that he neglects to ask himself what he can offer. As he cannot manifest contribution, he cannot experience completeness.

The man who reflects on being part of an infinite universe, approaches life with the thought: "How can I help and what can I offer?" That man enters the contribution process naturally, with a deep knowledge and awareness of his skills and talents. And by doing so, he appears as the natural leader because he thinks of his needs in terms of the needs of others. He is in a position to see the big picture and he is thus presented with ample opportunities. That man will receive the answers to the things he desires: he will hear about an excellent catering service at the time he is thinking of having a house gathering, or he will happen to meet someone who will give him valuable input regarding a project he has under way, etc. He considers others to be friendly and supportive. He also knows that his friends and relatives look out for him and want what is best for him. He is not jealous of others, because he understands that their efforts and successes will lead the way— of possibility—for the rest of them. Besides, he knows that in this abundant universe, he can unconditionally claim the things that he dreams about.

The man who knows he is part of an infinite universe, also knows that creative energy is always available and flows to and from him; manifesting as progress. He understands that the source of abundance lies within. He realizes that he cannot attain abundance with either offensive or defensive behaviors. He knows that there is no need to pressure things. All he needs to do is to align himself with the abundance that flows within him and allow people and situations to appear at the right time, with the perfect solution to what is happening.

The man who adopts a mindset of sufficiency and abundance sees himself as whole and complete. He knows that he is enough and he has enough. He feels excited about the possibilities and expects the best. He is thrilled and empowered.

It is important to recognize which behaviors are associated with deprivation:

- Do you look outside yourself and compare with others?

- Do you not appreciate what you have? Are you always searching for something else?

- Are you pursuing things in your environment in order to feel sufficient?

If that is your orientation, then you must choose to look in the opposite direction in order to feel:

- That right now, everything in life is sufficient

- Gratitude for all that you have

- Enthusiasm for all that you wish to experience and faith in their fulfillment

When you feel that you are being held back and cannot seem to understand why, just ask yourself whether you focus is on deprivation. In the event that your energy is negative, purposefully change it and embrace different thoughts with the help of the tools we provide below.

THE CHALLENGE YOU ARE ABOUT TO FACE

If you are not experiencing the kind of abundance you desire, now you know why: on account of your limiting beliefs and your restrictive action patterns. Whether you are short of money, or failing to enjoy health, love and success, it is because you keep bottled up inside certain beliefs that are contrary to attaining your goals. Why do you do that? For the simple reason, that you do not realize their impact on your life. Or it might be because you do not comprehend that those beliefs are invalid and they are nothing but mere interpretations of events, usually given by other people and not you. It is the way that your social surroundings (parents, friends, teachers, and relatives) perceive and understand situations and events, and because you think highly of those people, you therefore take their interpretation as a given.

But to identify your life with your convictions about life and to believe that this is the only way, can prove to be one of the biggest obstacles you have to confront.

The phrase, "I do not have enough" reflects one of the most inhibiting beliefs there is. When, however, people say that, they are actually saying that they are not enough, or otherwise they would have been able to attract a different reality (as per the Law of Attraction). But for that to happen, you have to train your mind to remove any thoughts of deprivation and restriction and instead focus on thoughts of sufficiency and abundance.

If your frame of thinking centers on deprivation and restriction, you are bound to receive an abundance of those qualities. The Law of Abundance works exactly the way it was designed to: to provide you with a plethora of the things you desire— through your conscious or subconscious thoughts and their resulting vibration. This goes to show you that if your thoughts are focused on deprivation and restriction, you will accordingly receive an abundance of deprivation and restriction.

Consequently, it is extremely important to gain awareness of what you think or talk about with yourself, at any given moment in time.

What kind of abundance, do you attract into your life?

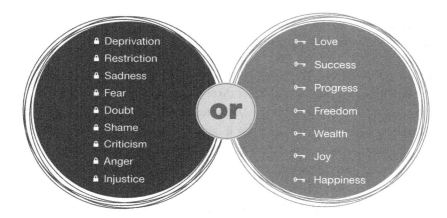

In order to better understand your natural tendency, you can check out the relevant tables in the Workbook which illustrate both the mindset of people who receive abundance in their lives and the mindset of those who receive deprivation. How about you? Which one is your orientation?

As long as you are able to grasp, as well as integrate the benefits of your actions which are driven by abundance, you will no longer be tempted to use your energy to pressure, force, coerce, contest, or demand your share. You will be certain that whenever you have a desire in your heart, there is always the possibility to fulfill it and that this is your birthright in life.

Of course, to change one's thoughts or beliefs can seem daunting or even impossible at times, but think of the following: a greater amount of energy is required to maintain your limiting beliefs—that antagonize your true self—than to change them.

Eventually, when you are in a position to love who you are right now and be satisfied with all that you have, while at the same time feel excited about the future, only then will you be in perfect alignment with the Law of Sufficiency and Abundance.

THE ULTIMATE GOAL IN APPLYING THE LAW

As a general rule, we must always differentiate between abundance and sufficiency. Abundance means that there is plethora of anything you want. Ergo, your goal should be plethora and not sufficiency.

Why is it so important to have plethora? Because when you do, you can keep something in reserve and that makes it possible for you to offer to other people as well. For it is true that only when you offer to others, can you attain absolute completeness. It also goes to show you why many wealthy people around the world have formed charities. Because they already apply the laws of creation and they know that contribution is the means to feel truly fulfilled.

APPLYING THE LAW OF SUFFICIENCY AND ABUNDANCE

Here are some practical suggestions to practice the application of the Law of Sufficiency and Abundance:

① SHOW GRATITUDE AND APPRECIATION FOR THE THINGS YOU ALREADY HAVE

The first step to embracing the energy of sufficiency and abundance is to be happy; pleased with what you have achieved so far, and excited about what the future holds. And to be thankful for what you have in your life right now.

If you are looking outside yourself, in hopes of external situations or circumstances helping you become more or who you think you are, you are obviously not living in the present and you are being unappreciative of the things you have. In case you were to expect something to happen, that would actually be construed as expecting something from outside to fill the void inside. This rationale would make you lose track of the present; which is all you have in the end.

If, on the other hand, your position on life sustains that what you have is enough, then clearly you are at peace. Besides, true happiness can only be found when you are grateful for the things you have now and excited for the things that the future will bring.

What do gratitude and appreciation signify? Why is it that they are so important?

Actually, gratitude and appreciation are among the highest energy vibrations. They are two of the noblest feelings that a man can experience, not to mention quite easy to attain. For instance, you cannot be in a place of deprivation (negative and low vibration) when you are feeling grateful (positive and high vibration). And because you cannot have two different vibrations at the same time, you can help yourself maintain and improve the higher vibration of the two.

Now, try and find things from your everyday life for which you are grateful: your house, your companion, your children, your job, your body, your health, your neighborhood, the sky, the flowers, your lunch, etc. Appreciate them and express your gratitude. Coordinate with those feelings and let them sweep you over. And just like that, you will open the door to the energy of abundance.

We already know that creation takes place when we feel content with where we are, while the same time, excited about the possibilities that lie ahead. You can use this knowledge and apply the law, by placing your hand on your heart and regularly repeating to yourself: "I am pleased with what I have!"

To be satisfied and grateful is the key to open the gate of universal abundance that will bring you love, time, compassion, opportunity, money, and many other positive experiences that lead to enhanced prosperity. Moving forward, you can better apply the necessary steps—which we will discuss later on—that will bring you closer to fulfilling your desires.

② DEFINE YOUR MOST PROFOUND INTENTION

Every goal we set is designed to arouse a particular feeling. In essence, that feeling constitutes our most profound intention. The goal, for example, does not involve money per se, but rather the feeling of stability, comfort and freedom that comes from having money. The aim is not the promotion itself, but the feeling of recognition and success that it produces. Similarly, the goal is not to find a companion, but to bring love, connection, and fulfillment to our lives; by means of a healthy, harmonious relationship.

It is, therefore, very important to define our deepest needs and goals for the purpose of gaining clarity on how we can better formulate our choice of action strategy.

The story that follows might help you make this distinction clearer.

A man wanted to make one million euro. To that end he worked very hard, always investing money in various business ventures. After ten years of being absolutely devoted to this strategy, he realized that he had not managed to gain enough and that, if he continued in this way, he would just end up wasting his life. At that point, he asked himself a very important question: what was his profound motive for wanting to make one million euro?

The answer he got was that he wanted time to do the things he enjoyed. So he decided to make time for himself in his everyday life. It was not long before he came to the realization that—if there was one thing missing—it was his self-esteem. Apparently, whenever something would come up at work, he would immediately stop what he was doing and would give up his free time for the sake of his job. That thought also made him realize that he always put others' needs ahead of his own. Therefore, he decided to stop doing that and to give himself priority.

Without knowing, he had already taken the three most basic steps: the realization that he was going about it the wrong way; using a strategy that was obviously not working, the recognition of his true objective and, last but not least, the acknowledgment of what hindered the manifestation of the result he desired. Now, he was ready to invest time in what he wanted.

He recalled that, in his youth, he used to play a musical instrument and that it gave him enormous pleasure. So he started playing again, and in time he felt inspired and went on to write his own music. He uploaded his recordings online and soon after a record company approached him for the copyrights to his music. Little by little, this activity prospered and before two years have passed, he managed to raise the one million euro—his earnings from selling his music to the theater— and his dream came true.

Apparently, by focusing on what he really wanted—experiencing the joy and relaxation of creative activity—this man was able to reach his goal; that is to raise the amount he wanted to, therefore, satisfy his inner most desire. But mind you, the money was only the end result and not the means.

This story goes to show you that as long as you accurately define your desires, you too will walk in the right path of creation. All you have to do is ask the right questions and seek out your true and -often unspoken- deliberate goals.

③ **SET YOUR GOAL AND IMAGINE HAVING ALREADY ACHIEVED THEM**

The secret to activate the Law of Sufficiency and Abundance lies in the ability to imagine and feel that what your soul desires is already yours. And that no matter what you yearn for, it has already come true.

The very act of wanting something—whether a job with benefits, a new and safe car, or a faithful and passionate companion—ensures that the result will always remain in the future. That is because, even the use of the verb "want" suggests that it is something that you do not presently have, but—best case scenario— hope to attain. In that respect, the message you are sending out to the universe, via your thoughts and vibration, conveys that you lack what you desire.

We already know that the universe will respond to our every thought, as reflection of our beliefs. For instance, if someone wants a new job, yet his thought remains in a state of longing, the universe will receive the message—lack of new job—and will answer: "Your wish is my command! I will give you lack of new job." And it will continue to do so for as long as you convey the same message. If, instead, you nurture your emotions to reflect the fulfillment of that which you desire, you will attract this result in a much more efficient way than prayer or longing could ever achieve. This vibration of completeness is communicated to the universe with phrases like, "I'm excited that my new job is on the way." The universe then mirrors that vibration and brings you similar actions in the form of situations or experiences related to fulfilling job prospects. Do you grasp the subtle but important difference?

How can you utilize that key to move from a place of deprivation to a place of abundance?

First, you must clearly identify what you want. Then, ask yourself: "How will I feel when this desire is fulfilled?" To illustrate, let us take the above example where you long for a new job. Now, imagine yourself presenting your ideas in front of an audience that is practically thrilled. How does that make you feel: successful? That you are finally recognized? No matter what your feelings are, indulge in them.

The trick is to live and breathe as if this is what you are experiencing right now. The more you implement the process, the easier it becomes and the better it feels. Visualizing it alone is not enough. You must let yourself feel that your desire is actually happening and allow the universe to work and do the rest.

If you want to find a love partner, let yourself get lost in the thought of being in his arms. How do you feel? Do you feel loved, appreciated, connected? If you want to have financial abundance, take your time to imagine the feeling of having more money than you could ever spend. Do you feel secure? Do you feel successful? Or even relieved? Feel it now! Feel whatever you want, with passion and purpose, and a breath of life will fill your body. Only when you feel that you already have what you want, will your desire come true.

As we said in the previous chapter, it turns out that your mind cannot distinguish between a thought and an actual occurrence. The mind is unable to make that distinction. Suffice to imagine it and align your vibration with the emotion it produces. The laws will only pick up your vibration and respond accordingly; nothing else.

Take two to four minutes a day to make a mental connection with your hopes and dreams. Become accustomed to that frequency vibration—through training—and observe how you gradually manage to tune in, with increasing ease and speed. Before long, that feeling will become permanent and the manifestation of your desire will shortly follow.

④ FOR A DIFFERENT RELATIONSHIP WITH MONEY

Money is also energy and as such it awaits your thoughts in order to take shape and form in your life. If you were to change your energy (thoughts and emotions) towards money, the energy that you receive would also change. Think of money as a medium, or simply an ally in achieving your goals. Think of it as guilt-free and concentrate on the positive feelings of abundance that it can bring to your life.

At the "http://www.trueme.co/" site you may find two useful tools to help you instantly form a better relationship with money. The first one is in regard to the meditation: "Create a relationship with money". If that interests you, please send a message to "mailto:info@trueme.co" to download it for free. You can find the second tool in the section of affirmations, along with suggestions about developing a dominant thought—a fitting statement—so that you start thinking about money in a different way. Of course, you can always adopt one of the statements already provided for you.

⑤ APPLY THE RULE OF ONE-TENTH

The rule of one-tenth refers to giving one tenth of your income, your time, or your talents to a benevolent cause. Regardless of your income level or your present conditions, you have to make sure that you offer something back, to a valued cause. It is not so much the quantity of what you give. It is more the satisfaction that you are adding value to the lives of others.

⑥ RELEASE ALL RESISTANCE TO THE FLOW OF ABUNDANCE

As you now know, the thing that stands between you and your desires—blocking the free energy flow of Well-being which contains abundance—is actually your thoughts and your limiting emotions. The kind of emotions that lead you to non-productive behaviors and actions, such as: resentment, envy, jealousy, self-pity, anger, criticism, cruelty, hatred, greed, laziness, arrogance, selfishness, grief, are feeling jealous or envious of someone, you are implying that what he has is not available to you. However, this contradicts the Law of Abundance. Your external reality cannot be separated from your internal reality. It is, therefore, necessary to recognize those feelings and to release them. That is the only way to allow for the energy of abundance and Well-being, that is already within you, to flow smoothly and uninterrupted.

⑦ CONTROL YOUR INNER DIALOGUE

The above give rise to the need to control your inner dialogue, whose role is not only important, but also strongly impacts your life. Holding on to negative emotions and not being able to understand the way to deal with them is a major obstacle to the fulfillment of your desires. Needless to say, it is important to become aware of the thoughts that your mind keeps on recycling—about yourself, other people, and life in general. Since you now have an even greater awareness, you can begin transforming that negative energy. To that effect, you have to practice in applying the information you learn here and the tools that you are given.

⑧ FORGIVE THOSE WHO HAVE WRONGED YOU

While forgiveness is perhaps one of the most difficult things to do, it is possibly one of the greatest gifts you can give yourself.

When we talk about forgiveness, we usually refer to the emotional relief from negative experiences and emotions caused to you by others. But there is also a different, more important, type of forgiveness and that is forgiving yourself for whatever choices you have made that caused pain to you or others.

The act of non-forgiveness recycles debilitating thoughts and emotions like: sadness, anger, resentment, or even the desire for revenge. However, we all are experienced enough to know that bitter thoughts cannot bring happiness or prosperity. When you become attached to those kinds of feelings, you only hurt yourself. No matter how justified you feel and despite what other people have done, clinging to the past holds you hostage to situations that are too far apart from a life of abundance.

When you insist on assigning blame on somebody else—by holding him responsible for your own feelings— you are basically handing your power over to him. Often, the behavior of other people in our lives strikes a chord or pushes our buttons, causing us to react in unpleasant ways. Nonetheless, you must realize that it was your mind which created those buttons to begin with. What other people did was not intentional, so you as might as well stop blaming them because it is not fair.

On the other hand, when we take responsibility for our feelings and reactions (as we have mentioned earlier) we become more capable to face the situations that arise.

At this point, it is important to clarify that forgiveness is not about tolerating troublesome situations or behaviors. Forgiveness does not mean that you will let another person's bad behavior to carry on. It means that you forgive him, you become emotionally detached, and you exonerate him. To take a stand and set healthy boundaries is one of the most powerful acts of love, not only for your own benefit, but for the sake of others as well. Bear in mind, that forgiveness is a mental process; it does not involve interacting with the other person. In fact, true forgiveness means freeing yourself from emotional attachment to pain— letting go of the negative energy that comes from experiencing difficult situations.

With forgiveness, you can release your negative feelings and begin the journey of ascent to a higher vibrational state. Unless you forgive yourself and others, you will not be able to understand the meaning of freedom or be able to live in the present. And this is especially important, because the present creates the future. If you recycle thoughts of the past, you will create a future that is similar to the past. If, however, you forgive yourself and others and concentrate on the present and on something new, then you will be able to create anything you like.

Your acts of forgiveness can begin today by adopting a new and empowering dominant thought, as in the following declarations:

o—π "I open the door to my heart and through forgiveness I walk towards love"

o—π "I change my thinking and the world around me changes"

o—π "the past is over and it has no power over me"

o—π "my present thoughts create my future"

o—π "as I forgive myself, it becomes easier to forgive others"

Do not forget that the choice is yours. You can either remain attached to bitterness, or lead a life of happiness and fulfillment. But if you choose to show forgiveness and generosity to yourself and others, you will gain access to the abundant energy flow of Well-being, and remain there.

⑨ LET YOURSELF BE OPEN TO RECEIVE

Many people define their worth by what they offer to others. They become so focused and involved with it, that they completely disregard their own needs and have difficulty accepting compliments and kindness from anyone.

Yet, it is important to understand that for the flow of abundance to remain open, it must be bidirectional: a two-way flow. You should be equally ready and able to give and to receive. You must also allow others to experience the joy of giving. Do not monopolize it. Think of the joy you feel when you offer and pass it on to others. It also provides an opportunity for you to train in the emotions that arise at acceptance of a gift: a kind word, an act of tender and care, or a material good. By the time you become familiar with these feelings, you will be ready to live in a world where abundance flows to your direction.

⑩ TAKE RESPONSIBILITY FOR YOUR LIFE

Many people spend their lifetimes waiting for things to happen. But this should not be the case. The one who makes things happen has to be you! When you take responsibility for your life, you automatically stop being a victim and you no longer blame others for your experiences. When you blame others, you lose control and you become weak. Consider it your responsibility to act in a productive manner and give yourself what you desire: an abundance of experiences and material goods.

We have repeatedly said that the outer world of situations and experiences is nothing short of a reflection of our inner world of thoughts and emotions. The more satisfied you are, the more you express your appreciation for life and the more you will receive similar experiences. As a matter of fact, this gentle shift will drastically change your point of attraction; instead of feeling anxious, you will now feel enthused. Instead of clinging to the thought of your desire—a thought that keeps you in a constant state of dissatisfaction—you are now focused and grateful for your life.

Step by step, you have to accept the fact that everything you need is already within you: having a successful career, finding the ideal partner, having the perfect body, becoming rich, etc. In other words, the knowledge that you are already sufficient helps you attract the experience of abundance.

Remember that abundance is an infinite flow of Well-being that is always available to you. To shift your awareness to that premise, will not only give you an immediate feeling of relief, but will also provide you with an empowering framework of thinking that allows you to attract anything you like.

Chapter 5
THE LAW OF PURE POTENTIALITY

Everything is possible.
All the resources,
the talents and the skills
required to create the life you desire,
exist within you.

DEFINITION OF THE LAW OF PURE POTENTIALITY

Our next law is the Law of Pure Potentiality. This law is based on the premise that the essence of our existence is clear, pure conscience. The source of all creation— with man being part of creation—is pure potentiality. In our external reality, pure potentiality manifests in the form of experiences. Everything around us, every single thing we observe or experience, originally existed as possibility or as thought/idea. Accordingly, creation is the clear and pure possibility that develops in the physical dimension.

Take a minute to comprehend the meaning of this truth. Pure potentiality is the field of all possibility, as well as the source of our emotional and material wealth. It is an essential energy of life that knows no boundaries and which gives us—provided we are internally connected—immediate access to every needed resource and to the creativity required to accomplish our dreams.

Once you realize that your inner self; the spirit that takes over your brain and body, is endowed with Pure Potentiality, you will be synchronized with the universe's power of creation. Everything will be possible and there will be unlimited creativity. Remember the words of Jesus Christ: "God created man in his own image." The intelligence that created everything in the universe is part of who we are—it is us!

That goes to show that when you come to the realization that your true self is one of absolute and pure possibility, you will be in a position to align yourself with the universe's power of manifestation and everything will become possible for you.

> ## Everything is possible
> ## Creativity is infinite

As the Law of Pure Potentiality asserts, the universe knows no boundaries. The potential of the universe and all living matter is unlimited. The only boundaries are the ones that you inflict, when you allow your inferior emotions—fear, doubt, uncertainty, mistrust, etc.—to get the best of you.

The source of all creation is the conscience—the pure energy that seeks manifestation. As soon as you realize that your true self is one with that pure and clear possibility, you will become aligned with the power of all creation.

Actually, man can achieve anything he puts his mind to. Everything starts with an idea. Look at your house, for example. Everything that is in there was originally someone's idea that got implemented. Every little thing which is now part of your everyday life—the wheel, the car, the airplane, the mixer, the elevator, the smart phone or the computer—are all products of an idea that someone once had (from the inexhaustible field of possibility) and then carried out. With that in mind, you can indefinitely expand the experiences you bring into your life, because just like Einstein said: "Imagination is more important than knowledge."

When you connect to clear and pure potentiality, you can restrain the powerful instinct of applying force and pressure to accomplish your goals. When you know that you are personally connected to the source of an infinite universe, anxiety disappears and confusion or discomfort gives way to serenity.

Likewise, once you are in sync with this law, you realize that the biggest achievements and successes are not the result of effort, pressure or coercion, but rather the fluid, magnetic qualities of grace and peace.

THE TWO FUNDAMENTAL EMOTIONS

Spiritual psychotherapy teaches us that there are only two basic emotions: love and fear. Love belongs to the spirit and fear belongs to Self (Ego). The Ego is focused on the image we have of ourselves. A basically wrong depiction of ourselves that we sustain as of childhood—when we still had no conscience of our own, nor personal judgment—handed down by our teachers, relatives, and our environment in general.

The Ego identifies with what we do, how we look, how we dress, the car we drive, who our neighbor is, whom we marry, how we bring up our children. And all these worldly identities become true through validation and control.

The Ego teaches us that our bodies, our jobs, our relationships, and our personal and material possessions define who we are. The Ego constantly criticizes and compares and makes us feel insufficient. If you continue to believe that this insufficiency holds true, then by all means that is what you will create.

If you go about your life upholding beliefs that support the existence of constraints, the Ego will feel fear and will pressure you to create situations whose sole goal is to acquire money, prestige, or power. These are precisely the things that the Ego needs in order to feel free. After all, the Ego was taught to apply this strategy and that is what it has been doing up until today. The Ego pursues things that are outside, to validate its existence.

Surely, at some point in your life, you have been in a situation where most of your experiences were positive (i.e. a time when you had money, great relationships, good social status, professional recognition, etc.). But what happened when, all of a sudden and with no previous warning, your life deprived you of one or more of those positive experiences? How did that make you feel?

In cases like these, most people lose themselves and their identity. They no longer know who they are or how to face challenges. That is because the foundation upon which they have built their lives is made of contingent experiences. For, the power of Ego exists only for as long as external conditions are present.

In order to find out who you really are, you have to be liberated from your identification with the Ego.

The Ego is based on false authority and the duration of its power is conditional on the object of reference being present. To better illustrate, let me give you an extreme example. In case you hold a specific title; you are the president of the country, the director of a company, or just have a lot of money, it is likely that the power you enjoy is derived solely from your title, your position, or your money. On account of that, there is a strong possibility that those experiences will only last for the time that the conditions exist. As soon as the title, the job, or the money disappears, so will the power and identity of the Ego.

Usually, we keep such a long distance between us and our true self that the Ego becomes our reference point. However, the Ego is not really who you are. The Ego is the image of yourself: your social facade. It is the role or the roles you play in the theater of life. And that social mask is always under the influence of what exists outside: situations, circumstances, people and things, as it requires the supply of external power to sustain itself. In fact, the Ego thrives when it receives the approval of others and when it dominates situations. But equally important, the Ego has a strong need to control things to ensure that the fear that lives within is also under control.

It holds true that most of us are focused on what is going on outside. You must, however, realize that by focusing on the external world, you are probably seeking validation from others. Your thoughts, your beliefs, your emotions and your behaviors are expecting the environment to respond, so that they can ascertain their value. Nevertheless, since you cannot control everything that takes place outside yourself, you fear, doubt and stress over what will actually happen and what will others say or think. And that way of thinking—that attitude—keeps you far away from the life of Pure Potentiality.

Conversely, when we live our lives through the power of our inner self, there is an absence of fear and we do not feel compelled to either control things or struggle to get other peoples' approval. The opinions and actions of others have no bearing on us and therefore we do not need them in order to feel validated. Your true, inner self is completely free from such behaviors. It is immune to criticism; fearless in the face of challenge and feels inferior to no one. At the same time, however, the inner self is modest and does not feel superior to any one either, because it recognizes that every person is a unique spiritual being. When your spirit is your reference point, you experience your true existence. That is the basic difference between focusing on the inner self and focusing on the Ego.

The power of the inner self is permanent, since it is based on knowledge of the spirit. The spirit neither compares nor competes, given that we are all different but at the same time connected. Since the spirit does not know fear—only love—it does not feel threatened by any situation of life. Criticism cannot hurt it either. When you go through life with the power and energy of the spirit, you are connected with pure potentiality and the foundation of your life is stronger than before. You only attract the people and the situations you want; the ones that can support you in fulfilling your desires. You also invite the support of the laws of the nature. You have such strength that you can have an intimate bond with people and people can have an intimate bond with you. Your power derives from connection; a connection that comes from true love. Think of it this way: why operate on rechargeable batteries, when you can simply connect directly to the infinite energy flow of the universe?

When you abide by the Law of Pure Potentiality, you can achieve a profound transformation of your perception of life, the perception of others and yourself. You will no longer see the world as a place of struggles and endless ordeals, but rather a place of comfort and co-creation that is limitless and exciting. Accordingly, you will change your perception that people can be obstacles or threats, inferior or exhausting, as from now on you will attract people who are kind, resourceful, respectful and trustworthy. Whereas before you constantly felt overwhelmed, depressed, stressed, and out of balance, you will now feel empowered, creative, connected, relaxed, focused, confident, strong and safe.

INTERNAL CONNECTION – ACTIVATION OF THE FEMALE ENERGY

Regardless of gender, there are two kinds of energy in each one of us: the male and the female. The female energy is directed to the inner self and is cooperative and co-creative. On the other hand, the male energy has an outward orientation and is based on the power of force and action. And while the male approach requires great physical, mental and emotional effort, the female energy allows us to achieve more with less stress and less struggle.

Whenever you are in search of something that you want—whether it is a new job, a new partner, a new car, or a more joyful and creative life—you have two alternatives.

You can either use your male energy to hunt, entrap and acquire that what you want, or use your female side; that turns to your inner self and uses the energy that lies therein to magnetize whatever you want. The female approach is the one that allows you to connect with the infinite Pure Potentiality and to achieve vibrational alignment with the results you want.

When you learn to rely on the female power that exists within, you will be able to produce the most inspiring results with more joy and less effort. You will always be determined to attain your goals. But now you can be even more effective in doing so, provided you connect with and mirror your inner strength, instead of imposing it. Perhaps the female approach seems more passive to you. Maybe, even less effective than the male approach that is action-oriented, but consider this practical aspect: why work hard and always struggle when there is no need for it?

Undeniably, to establish a strong, internal connection is the fastest way to align your personal energy with the infinite intelligence of the universe. The stronger the connection and the more confidence you have in yourself, the less likely you are to feel the need to change the prevailing conditions. When deep inside you know that the energy of all creation is flowing from and towards you, you realize how pointless it is to waste it by trying to push for change.

As you learn to move forward in acknowledgment of the power of this high level consciousness, you will better understand that you are not someone who has to fight tooth and nail for what he wants. You are the child of an abundant universe where everything is possible, and that you too possess the ability to create anything you desire. And while many people go through life planning and pressuring situations, the empowered and enlightened man draws them like a magnet; because his approach is filled with the grace of the universe.

At this point, it is important that you realize that what determines the outcome is the assembly and alignment of your energy, and not the extent of your effort.

It is true that, sometimes, the male approach makes us aggressive, makes us go to extremes or lose our patience. But when we embrace also the female approach, we sense that the struggle is coming to an end and that the storm subsides. And we regain the feeling that life is flowing, even when things are not going our way.

You must realize that peace does not exist because of change. It comes only when you understand and love who you are. Accordingly, you have to withdraw your attention from the outer world of possessions and achievements and ground yourself on your own inner strength. In that way, you will see your vibration releasing the tension, becoming clean, calm, and focused.

Only when you reach for the deeper levels of your existence, can you change your life and the lives of others around you.

THE ESSENCE OF YOUR EXISTENCE

You must learn to get in touch with the innermost essence of your existence. Your true essence lies beyond the Ego. You are fearless and you are free. You are also immune to criticism. Challenges do not intimidate you. You are not inferior to anyone, you are not superior to anyone; you are full of magic, mystery and charm.

You can easily understand—through your relationships—whether you have access to your true self, since all the relationships you form are but reflections of your connection with yourself.

For example, if you feel guilt, fear and insecurity over money, success, or anything else, then those feelings are obviously reflections of the guilt, fear and insecurity you feel in relation to yourself. No amount of money and no rate of success will be enough to resolve those fundamental existential problems. The only, real cure is intimacy with your self. Because when you rely on the knowledge of your true self— when you really understand your true nature— you will no longer feel guilty, afraid, or insecure about money, success, or the fulfillment of your desires. You will come to realize that the essence of all material wealth is the energy of life: Pure Potentiality. When you know that you are part of a universe that will provide you with everything you need, then you become unlimited in your potential. Pure Potentiality is the inherent nature of us all.

When you are in harmony with your possibilities, there is no fear, and that is when you feel deeply and truly free!

You are fearless

You are free You fear no challenge

You are inferior to no one You are superior to no one

You are full of magic and charm

You are love

The deepest essence of your existence

When you are focused on your inner self, you not only feel more peaceful and relaxed, but you automatically connect with your intuition. You connect with the part of yourself that is full of wisdom and is one with the superior intelligence of life. On instinct, you can recognize and avoid situations that keep you away from your desires. And, at the same time, you can take action that leads you directly to the fulfillment of your goals. This action we call inspired, because it derives from your inner wisdom and not the Ego. From this secure, internal base you will become better parents, better partners, better lovers and friends and you will transmit vibrations of internal peace that everyone will be able to feel. Instead of working on your own, struggling to bring the results you want, you can start cooperating with the Universe to co-create a wonderful life.

APPLYING THE LAW OF PURE POTENTIALITY

Below you may find some practical suggestions on how to shift focus to your inner self.

① THE PRAYER

If you are a man of prayer, possibly you are already employing the Law of Pure Potentiality; believing in a higher spirit or God as the source of everything. Surely, that provides you with an advantage. You have had practice with talking to the source of all energy.

If, however, this approach has not brought you peace, you should probably change the way you pray. If you are driven by fear or doubt, or use a demanding tone when you pray; often asking, "Why me?", then you're far from aligning with the energy of the higher spirit and applying the Law of Pure Potentiality.

On the other hand, if faith guides you and you use it to clearly express your gratitude for your present situation, your wishes, and your requests; you are definitely in alignment with the energy of creation.

② MEDITATION

Practicing meditation is yet another way to achieve alignment with the energy of creation. Meditation is the state in which you rest your mind and all thoughts of resistance—that would otherwise prohibit the vibrational alignment with your source—automatically stop. By listening to the source—via the meditation technique— you establish a connection with pure potentiality.

There is no room for fear in that process either.

You may begin your meditation by choosing to repeat some of the affirmations contained in the Workbook. When you are ready, find a quiet place, close your eyes and repeat your affirmations while taking deep breaths.

Another way to meditate is the following: direct your attention to the flame of a candle, observe it for as long as you can, and try to create silence in your mind, fending off gently all possible thoughts.

Or, if you prefer, you can use a guided meditation, like the ones found on the website HYPERLINK "http://www.trueme.co/" \h www.trueme. co. There, you can also find more information about the art of meditation and its positive impact.

Start off with something simple and go slowly. In the beginning, five minutes are enough to become accustomed to being alone with your self.

As you progress, I suggest you spend twenty to thirty minutes, morning and night. Anyway, you can start anywhere you like and proceed from there.

Apply whatever technique agrees with your present level or works best for you. Do it systematically and connect as often as possible with your true inner self, pure potentiality, and the source. Indulge in it and observe yourself as it slowly enters into another field of vibration. You will discover that your feelings are beginning to change. You will feel serenity, peace and clarity and you will be ready to move on to effective and positive creation.

③ ABSTINENCE FROM CRITICISM

Another way to access the field of pure potentiality is through the practice of non-judgment. Criticism is the endless assessment of things as right or wrong, good or bad. When you do nothing but evaluate, classify, identify and analyze, you create turmoil in your internal dialogue. Consequently, turmoil obstructs the flow of energy between you and pure potentiality. When you refrain from judging, controlling and manipulating, when you are just love, then you behave like the source.

To aid yourself use the statement: "Today I will not criticize anything that happens." Indeed, lack of judgment will restore the silence in your mind. It is, therefore, a good idea to start your day with that statement and repeat it every time you realize that you are somewhat tempted.

If you think that full day practice is hard to achieve, you can just tell yourself: "For the next two hours I will not criticize anything" and gradually try to prolong that period. Try it, to immediately feel pure and light, and to restore peace in your life.

④ CONTACT WITH NATURE

Come into contact with nature and observe the intelligence that exists within every living creature. How do you feel when you watch the sunrise, when you listen to the waves crashing onto the rocks, or when you smell a beautifully-scented flower? All these and more were created by the infinite source: Pure Potentiality. Make time every day to get in touch with the energy of nature. To understand how the harmonious interaction of all life's elements and forces gives you a sense of unity with them. Whether it is a flower, a bird, a ravine, a forest, a mountain or the sea, the connection with the intelligence of nature will help you access the field of pure possibility. Your communication with nature and your silence will make you appreciate creativity's unlimited range of possibilities and feel the pulse of life throughout the centuries.

By forming a constant and permanent connection with your inner self, you introduce a new rhythm to your life that allows things—easily and naturally—to take their rightful place, in perfect timing. When you are connected to the fields of infinite possibilities, the magic begins to unfold.

As in the words of Lao Tzu: "Conquering others takes force, conquering yourself is true strength."

When you are in harmony with the Law of Pure Potentiality, you feel peaceful in the center of your core. You are unlimited, and you know only love. Fear does not exist and everything is possible.

When you know the truth about yourself, when you know you are an extension of the source or the higher spirit; when you recognize that you are made in the image and likeness of God, then you know that you can make all your dreams come true.

In view of every conscious decision, you should think, speak, and act using thoughts, words and actions that are in harmony with love. Try to behave like the source. That you can accomplish when you do not judge, do not control and do not manipulate.

Chapter 6
THE LAW OF DETACHMENT

To detach from desires results
in their accomplishment.

DEFINITION OF THE LAW OF DETACHMENT

According to the Law of Detachment, in order to be able to attain anything in the physical field, you must let go of your attachment to it. In other words, in order to successfully attract what you want, you need to emotionally disconnect.

That does not mean it is not legitimate to want things and to set goals for obtaining them. That means that, while you set your goals and proceed with necessary action, you refrain from being emotionally attached either to the particular method employed or the result itself.

> **In order to be able to attain anything in the physical Universe you have to let go of your attachment to it.**

When I say you should be emotionally detached, I mean that you should not think of your life, your value, or your progress being contingent on the outcome of any event. Instead, you should realize that life is a journey of learning and growth and that every experience adds to it.

The Law of Detachment refers to abandoning the need for control, whether it regards events, people, or desires.

Most people are troubled by the order of things; having to first choose their targets and then apply the Law of Detachment is a task they find quite difficult. Because of what they have been taught to believe, namely, that success only comes as a result of achieving goals, they will do practically anything to achieve those goals. They believe that, only if certain conditions exist (i.e. get good grades at school, study at a particular university, marry someone special, or have a senior level job), can they consider themselves successful—and more importantly—can they be considered successful by others. And so they pressure, exploit and degrade themselves and others until they get the results they want. In case they do not succeed, and therefore fail to receive the outside validation they need, they become anxious or confused, and end up losing themselves. Because they have never learned, or realized for that matter, that true value lies within and is not determined by either acts or achievements, or by the people who surround them; even if they surround them with love. When you forget your true self, which is pure conscience and possibility, you begin to feel that you need something outside yourself to make you happy. You presume that you will feel good when you have a million euros in the bank, when you lose twenty pounds, when you find your soul mate, and so on. Actually, in all those cases, you have placed your power on something outside yourself, thinking that it will determine your happiness. But then again, that frame of mind cannot support you on a regular basis, because whatever exists outside yourself could be lost at any moment.

Having understood who you are now—at the core of your existence—you know that you are part of the universe, that abundance is yours and that you have limitless possibilities.

As of this moment, you are ready to indulge with faith in the journey of life, while being flexible in your methods and keeping an open mind to pursue every possible path that may lead to the results you desire.

You are now able to realize that if you are fixated on achieving a goal (i.e. improving your finances, finding a partner, acquiring the home you want, or getting the scores you need to get into the university) you might exhibit feelings of fear, doubt or longing that will actually attract the opposite of your desire. Likewise, if you worry, fear or doubt, you will cancel out the power of request, and you will fail to receive the things you want, yet again.

Keep in mind that neither luck nor coincidence exist. You therefore need to work with the Law of Attraction to create what you want. Also, it is important to know that, in the creative process, the Law of Detachment is the flip side of the coin. Specifically, the Law of Detachment provides the necessary supplementary action for the Law of Attraction to work, and makes a huge difference in its application.

Detachment is made possible when you have an abundant consciousness; a consciousness that allows you to trust and know that, when the time is right, everything will take its perfect place. You already know—from the Law of Pure Potentiality—that you can be, do, and have anything you want in your life. With the Law of Detachment, you will learn to trust and be confident that the best things can and will happen to you.

Clinging to things, as an attitude of life, has its price. Your conscious or unconscious desire to uphold this standpoint derives from your own need to feel safe and secure. It comes from the fear of the unknown. Nevertheless, it is a tactic that makes you weak. Because, in essence, it automatically puts an end to all evolution. And when there is no evolution, there is stagnation, entropy, disorder and decay. For the simple reason, that lack of evolution is contrary to human nature. It opposes the higher needs of development and progress. And when man fails to meet his needs, he cannot reach the level of fullness and completion that his soul craves.

On the contrary, being detached from the outcome you expect shows real power, knowledge and understanding of how things work in life. It means that you have learned to trust.

If I would attempt to define the meaning of trust, I would say that it is the certainty and knowledge that you will receive what you need. Not necessarily what you think you want—which derives from the Ego—but the thing that really matters to you and that which is in in tune with the reality of your existence.

In order to apply the Law of Detachment, you must follow the creative process below: ask for what you want, focus on what is important, take action on what is in your control and move on to achieve the things you want. The rest is up to the universe. You know well that the results will come. You also have to believe that they will come when the time is right. So, stop worrying, stop feeling nervous and discard every doubt and negative thought.

Otherwise, if you try to create something with lack of trust; feeling insecure, afraid, or in doubt of your ability to succeed, you hinder the efficiency of the universe's energy flow: in short you create resistance.

As long as you are attached to a particular outcome, you define happiness and completeness as conditional probabilities. You are looking outside yourself for situations, events and people to assign them the role of your source of happiness and your source of fulfillment, respectively. Actually, the object of your attachment—the one that you think will make you happy or unhappy—deprives you of your power. Similarly, when you look outside yourself for strength and happiness, you identify something other than your true self as the source. But since you do not really have control over anything or anyone else, you put yourself at risk and become powerless.

Attachment always creates insecurity. No matter how much of what you want, you already have. Usually, the most insecure people are those who have more than they need, because they constantly worry about whether they will be able to keep it (i.e. their financial comfort, their partner, their health, etc.) or end up losing it.

——— DETACHMENT ———

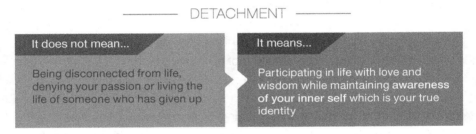

It does not mean...	It means...
Being disconnected from life, denying your passion or living the life of someone who has given up	Participating in life with love and wisdom while maintaining **awareness of your inner self** which is your true identity

After you determine what you want with absolute clarity, place it in the hands of the universe—the source of all energy. Indulge in the grace of this higher power; always working with you and through you for the greater good. Detach yourself and realize that all good comes from the spirit and nothing from the Ego. Just make sure that you uphold the right beliefs, the ones that permit the free flow of your desires. When you show trust, it means you are convinced that you are secure and that whatever happens is for your own good. The fact that you do not know when and how things will happen does not worry you, because you are certain that your desire will manifest.

The source of all good things, such as joy and abundance, is your higher self and any attachment indicates separation.

Conversely, in detachment lies the wisdom of uncertainty, and in the wisdom of uncertainty lies the freedom from the known—your experience to date, the past. In your willingness to step into the unknown, you surrender to the creative mind that orchestrates the universe. With doubt and fear, you stand in the way of the energy that creates the result and in doing so you block its efficient flow.

The elements of uncertainty and the unknown constitute the field of all possibility which is always timely, new and open to creation. When faced with uncertainty, it means that you are on the right track, so do not give up. When your perspective on how things evolve is rigid or inelastic, it shows that you are attached to it and so you rule out a whole range of other possibilities.

The universe responds way better at times when you feel relaxed, in terms of your goals. That is when you are neither desperate nor obsessed. On the other hand, when you say or think, "I must get the ...," or "If I don't get .... I will have failed," you undeniably lock your mind in a stable and rigid mode.

The ease and perfection of action depends solely on the degree to which you stop depending on the rational of your mind: the Ego. You need to silence the conscious mind for the subconscious to take over. The pilot and the autopilot cannot simultaneously fly the plane. You should turn off the autopilot (conscious) in order to let the actual pilot (subconscious) gain control.

To be detached means that you allow the universe to bring you your desire in the best way possible. When you are detached, your desires manifest more quickly.

When you become adept at this law, you will be able to maintain an unshakable calm and be in a position to passionately devote yourself to the goal.

It is important to understand that, although your intent concerns the future, your attention has to be kept on the present. Only on that condition, can your future intent manifest. Since intentions create reflections on the outside world, vibrations that are positive in nature and in harmony with your intentions will allow you to proceed, in confidence, with the realization of your desires.

Whenever situations do not seem to evolve the way you like them to, it is because a negative vibration is present; something you can easily perceive from the way you feel (as stated in the relevant chapter).

In the event that you already have mastered the Law of Detachment, your perception widens and generates a more essential experience: individual attention extends to cosmic attention. You can now see the natural world through the eyes of the spirit. The wisdom of uncertainty prevents you from pursuing static moments and everything works perfectly. Every situation brings with it the seed of opportunity. Each experience denotes excitement, adventure and mystery. Feel free to embrace the moment and enjoy the unexpected result of this action: the birth of the idea; the epiphany. It is a quantum leap towards the creation of your desires.

The Law of Detachment accelerates the whole process of evolution. When you come to truly comprehend this law, you will no longer feel the need to impose solutions or put pressure on situations and people. And that is legitimate, because when you force a solution to a problem, you only provoke similar situations.

When you show patience and faith, the right solution will manifest. Do not be discouraged if you get confused somewhere along the way. Confusion is right before clarity; it is the stage where your mind is in search of a solution.

Give yourself time and you will find that it will open the gateway to new understanding. From chaos there will be order.

With everything you already know, you can understand that detachment is yet another way to implement the Law of "Allowing". It is the ultimate act of consent. It means that you let go, surrender to whatever happens, while believing and remaining focused on your goal without, however, clinging to a specific action strategy or a specific outcome. You only have to be aware of the essence of your desire and show confidence in the ability to experience it. When you are in harmony with the Law of Detachment, you no longer have to push for things to happen, you just let them be. When you allow, you are in vibrational alignment with ultimate creation and things flow in your direction in a harmonious and uninterrupted manner.

Accordingly, express your intentions—steering clear from the results—and your wishes will come true. The more you detach, the sooner you will receive the things you want. Besides, inside every challenge and every difficulty lies the greatest potential for growth. When you trust the universe, anything is possible.

DISCONNECT FROM SHORTAGE AND SHOW FLEXIBILITY

You cannot create from a position of shortage. You must be in a position of positive expectation. All of us have experienced situations where the more we tried to accomplish something, the worse things became. So stop with the pressure. When the universe works, everything is so much easier. The universe can manage situations that you cannot. It is preferable to rely on the universe, than on your own strength. Whatever is under your control, by all means control it. Whatever is out of your control, let the source handle it. When you trust the source, everything works out fine.

The universe will never deny your request; you will always be able to create what you want for yourself. But in order to experience lack of resistance and the effortless achievement of goals, you have to willfully surrender to the flow of energy that only wants what is best for you.

Consider the following: you are in point A and you plan to get to point B. Between points A and B there are infinite paths, infinite possibilities. By applying the Law of Detachment–with the addition of uncertainty in the equation—you can at any time change direction, find a higher ideal or another destination that is worth pursuing.

In this way, you will adopt an attitude that does not try to force specific solutions on problems, and this will allow you to remain open and alert to new opportunities. Even if one door is closed, you will find another one which is open. In some way or another, you can always get what you want, provided you remain positive and receptive to whatever solution is presented.

Imagine that you are searching for a job and that you are currently in the phase of interviews for a position that seems to meet your expectations. As you successfully proceed with the interviews, everything indicates that the odds are in your favor. At the last moment, however, they go and hire someone else. If you already know how to apply the Law of Detachment, you will remain calm, because you know that another, more suitable opportunity will soon come your way. If, however, you now feel stressed and confused about how things turned out, it implies that you were attached to the thoughts of getting that job. You probably thought that this particular job was either the only solution to your problem or the only way to satisfy your needs.

Do not get involved in a situation, if you feel that it is your only option. That is when you are most likely to become attached. In the event that what you want to do is for some reason not readily available, you might be disappointed and lose the vibrational alignment with your center. For your own sake, you should have a lot of good options, available in case you need them. When that is the way you lead your life, it is highly probable that you will get what you want, since the vibration of your energy is the right one.

Familiarize yourself with the thought that:

- there is an infinite intelligence, working alongside your intelligence, which can bring you a better outcome or a more worthy experience

- all you have to do is to declare your intentions and desires, and detach yourself from the how and when they will occur

THE ROLE OF GOALS

To detach does not mean to give up or abandon your goals. It is necessary for you to have goals, otherwise you deny your internal desires and you cut yourself off from development and progress. Goals inspire you to live, to create, and to move forward. If you fail to grow, you wallow in stagnation. It is important for you to want to embrace desires and intentions. But you should refrain from clinging to them. It is natural to want to implement your goals and desires—we all want to. But if you consider their achievement as the source of prosperity, happiness or self-worth, then you have already failed.

That is the reason why detachment is of such vital importance. When it is not necessary to accomplish your goal in order to feel good or happy, then you can simply enjoy the process. Because in that process lie happiness, expansion and growth. You will have noticed that at the moment you accomplish a goal, you start setting new ones. The implementation of a single goal alone does not bring completeness. Once a goal is attained, you will move forward—by virtue of evolution—in search of your next target.

In no way, can the accomplishment of your objectives be the source of your peace of mind, or the source of your fulfillment; especially in the long run.

Clearly, the purpose of life is growth. Life without growth becomes unbearable. It is the cycle of continuous progress that makes us happy. We are energy beings and energy is always in motion. We live, therefore, we constantly move and flow. Nothing is static. We either progress or regress, but we never remain still. Unless we grow spiritually, we feel as if we die. Unless we expand, we collapse.

Therefore, do not condemn yourself to a standstill. Sooner or later you will realize that it is not in your best interest, because stagnation can bring about depression, hopelessness, or even illness. You should, instead, let yourself freely flow towards exciting goals, enjoy the journey, and let the universe do the rest.

ENLIGHTENMENT

Enlightenment is a state of non-attachment. It is the realization that all difficulties appear when you spend energy on what you cannot control. Being detached gives you emotional freedom and psychological stability. Let your thoughts flow, because as long as there is flow, there is abundance. The moment you stop, anywhere along the line, you become stagnant and you go into a state of shortage. If, on the contrary, you manage to remain in a state of development, your intelligence and your knowledge will stay in force. But when you become attached, it appears that your intelligence and knowledge are of no effect.

Detachment is neither indifference nor apathy. Instead, it makes you feel that the universe protects you and you are confident that everything you want is already yours.

APPLYING THE LAW OF DETACHMENT

If you choose to adopt that frame of thought, you will be able to realize that every problem you face in your life is an opportunity to gain valuable knowledge, which you may have not had before. Every problem is an experience that offers a lesson. One that entails a new, valuable awareness that will raise the knowledge of your soul as a whole and which will enable you to conquer a higher level of existence and life experiences. It is, however, contingent on open mindedness and lateral thinking. By expanding your perception and remaining flexible, you will find the solutions you are looking for.

The Law of Attraction tells us that everything we experience is the result of what we sense and feel. We also know that when we have unwanted feelings, we attract undesirable experience.

I now want you to understand that when you experience unwelcome emotions, it is because you are in a state of attachment to certain things, people, or events that produce these feelings.

Let go of your attachment and stop worrying. Have no concern; just proceed as if it makes no difference whether your desire materializes or not. In that way, your feelings will allow for more positive vibrations that will draw creation, recognition, happiness and peace to your life.

The Law of Deliberate Creation, that is when you express your intention, and the Law of Detachment work together to create your desires. By engaging into deliberate creation, you go into a state of calm expectation: believing that what you want is already yours. Insofar as you become attached and are in doubt of your ability to create, your focus remains on the negative aspects of the things you do not want, and you will continue to feel fear.

To apply the Law of Detachment to any goal, you must show flexibility in the how and when: how you can accomplish it and when can you receive your desire. You should not hang onto a single strategy or a single solution. Have confidence in the universe and it will deliver to you something that is unexpected; something that is in harmonious vibration with you. Nevertheless, it is different and possibly even better than what you had in mind.

At this point, I must once again emphasize that detachment means freedom. There is no anxiety in detachment. Nor are there feelings of confusion and inconvenience. There is only relaxation and peace, since you know that no matter what the outcome is, it will be just perfect. It is common knowledge that the best possible solution will come. For the simple reason that detachment allows the universe to bring you something that exceeds your imagination.

In other words, have no worries. Just remember that there are no limits and no restrictions. Keep in mind that you have nothing to lose. So, go ahead and set your goals, take action, and observe how situations evolve in your favor.

Chapter 7
THE LAW OF POLARITY

Within each state there is an
inherent solution.
Focusing on the empowering
interpretation of situations leads
to a life of expansion.

DEFINITION OF THE LAW OF POLARITY

In this chapter, we will examine the Law of Polarity that states:

Unity is plural at a minimum of two

In duality, everything has two poles or two opposites. Polarity denotes both extremes. For example, temperature has two poles: the warm and the cold. The degrees along the rod measure each individual's perception of warm and cold. Warm and cold may mean different things to different people, much like rich and poor, love and hatred, good and bad, success and failure, beauty and ugliness, and so on.

Everything in the universe has an opposite. For example, your body has a right side and a left side; the front and the back. Every top has a bottom and every bottom has a top. The Law of Polarity states not only that there is an opposite of everything, but also that this opposite is proportional. Accordingly, if the distance from the ceiling to the floor is ten feet, the distance from the floor to the ceiling is also ten feet. Likewise, if the distance from Athens to Corinth is fifty-one miles, the distance from Corinth to Athens is also fifty-one miles.

The role of polarity in our lives seeks to enhance our experience. Because if it were not for polarity, how would you perceive good if, for example, evil did not exist? In the event that deprivation and restriction did not exist, how would you know what it is to live in abundance? If there was no failure, how would you recognize success? And if there was no death, how would you come to appreciate life?

The Law of Polarity encompasses a comprehensive range of possibilities that go from positive to negative with many fluctuations. So I am asking: where on the spectrum are you going to stand in order to handle the situation at hand? The choice—conscious or unconscious—is yours and it depends on your personal value and belief system and your experiences to date.

When the references in this book become part of your experience, you will come to accept and submit to any event that may occur in your life, knowing that facts are simply facts and the impact they have on your life depends solely on your attitude towards them. In time, you will learn to control your choices and will be able to shape, to form, and to live the life you consciously want. Regardless of your current perception of your life's situations, events, and circumstances, you will be able—one step at a time—to expand your understanding and realize that everything that happens is designed to enhance your natural experience and achieve your ultimate goal.

The Law of Polarity bears a great gift: the knowledge that, in spite of your former life experiences, you now have the ability and the potential to experience harmony and completeness in every area of your life. Because, with the knowledge you have gained, in case something bad happens you can seek out the good that is in it.

"IT JUST IS"

Consider the above phrase. Allow it to represent whichever situation you want. Reflect on the idea that every situation just is. It is you who can render it negative or positive, based on how you perceive it. The Law of Polarity attests to the fact that every situation is subject to multiple interpretations, within a range that extends from very negative to very positive, and vice versa. If you are currently experiencing a situation in such a negative way that it makes you weak, you can change your perspective, view it from the opposite angle and discover that it has a positive side or manifestation. Once you do this, you will understand that there is also a different way of doing things, and you will feel empowered.

Consequently, every possible situation has its opposite, which you have to look for in case it is not obvious. I trust you realize what a huge relief that knowledge is. It is very important to know that if you are faced with a seemingly difficult situation, you need only to look at it from a different angle to get a completely different experience. You just have to be willing to do it.

The Law of Polarity can be easily applied to your relationships with other people. If you feel that people around you want to take advantage of you, or that they do not understand and are either unfaithful or malicious, your relationships will be difficult and unsatisfactory. However, if you believe that all people do the best they can and you search for the good in them; not only will you greatly facilitate your existing relationships, but you will also attract new people who will enrich and enhance your experiences in life.

WHAT IS YOUR ORIENTATION?

Consider the following: There is an axis called natural health and wellness. In the negative pole there is illness and in the positive pole there is health. People who are all the time facing the negative pole—with the thought that they might get sick—often do. That is because the energy, resulting from their permanent focus, is in tune with these types of situations which—by virtue of the Law of Attraction—are therefore constantly recycled. On the contrary, people who constantly face the positive pole of health and wellness are likely to have developed certain dietary and exercise habits that allow them to always remain strong and fit.

In a similar scenario, people frequently stare at the pole of "I do not know what I want." These are people who concentrate either on the presence of the things they do not want, or the absence of the things they want. That focus will eventually create a vibrational separation between them and their inner self— that always searches for what it wants. The separation per se is what causes all the negative experiences. On the other hand, people who focus intensely on what they want will be able to eventually create the connection between them and their inner self. And in so doing, they will attract and recycle the experiences they aspire to have.

Every negative situation which you encounter has a corresponding positive or alternative side. Although there are thousands of practical options along the way, most of you—out of habit—continue to pick the prospect of scarcity and deprivation, misery and pain. This approach will make you end up in an undesirable place, where there are no more options, nor the possibility to gain access to something better.

When you intend to acquire Well-being, success, health, happiness and prosperity, you should align yourself with the energy frequency of such conditions. Because, given their positive vibration, they will ultimately prevail in your life.

When you happen to find yourself in extremely adverse conditions, the power that comes from within is very strong. On condition that you shift the focus of your power to the other side of the axis—the positive side—you will be able to reach a much higher energy level that will exalt you.

In other words, one who is very sick is more likely to become well than someone who is less sick, for the reason that the first man's desire for recovery is extremely strong and enlarged. The same applies to one who is very poor, very lonely, very scared, or desperate. There are numerous examples of people who managed to build empires from absolute poverty. And of people who albeit the once loss of loved ones, went on to create big and lovely families.

Obviously, in order to achieve those results they had to reverse their focus: from negative and discouraging to positive and empowering. In other words, those people eagerly sought health and distanced themselves from the notion of disease, they passionately sought abundance and walked away from the idea of poverty, or they deeply sought connection and withdrew from the meaning of loneliness, and so on.

THE SIGNIFICANT MESSAGE OF THE LAW OF POLARITY

On condition that you have fully grasped the message of this law, you will never again feel sad, doubtful or anxious. You will come to realize that no matter the kind of experiences you have had so far, you now have the ability and capacity to experience harmony and completeness in every field of your life. In that respect, anything that you perceive as a problem has an inherent solution. Every failure encompasses success, every sorrow encompasses happiness, and every deprivation encompasses abundance. And this is how it is, as long as you turn and knowingly face the positive pole of the axis of life.

You have learned from the Law of Attraction that any vibration you emit—with your energy, focus and attention—will come back to you, whether you like it or not. In a similar way to a boomerang1 that always returns to the person who threw it. And as a result, you will get more of the same vibration; a vibration that creates your experiences.

The dominant thought—your basic focal point—functions in essence as the seed for the harvest. Whatever you sow you will reap. To be able to experience positive events, situations, and circumstances you must sow positive thoughts; thoughts of faith, joy and excitement about the endless possibilities that unfold before your eyes. And of course you have to set your focus on the positive side of life's experiences.

The ability to experience the opposite of what displeases you is always available. The only thing that determines the results in your life is the way you choose to perceive and interpret events. Between two seemingly opposite experiences, there is only your notion of that which is right and your choice of focus.

Actually, you have freedom of choice to experience whichever end of the polarity spectrum you like. If you perceive your present situation as unpleasant, all it takes is for you to change what is in your mind (thoughts and beliefs) that created those unpleasant conditions to begin with.

And although we define that as the only condition to reach your goals, the procedure itself is demanding and time consuming and should not be taken lightly. At the same time, however, it is also precious and fascinating, since it frees you from the misleading tactics of the past that have kept you away from your desires.

1 boomerang noun: a bent or curved piece of tough wood used by the Australian Aborigines as a throwing club, one form of which can be thrown so as to return to the thrower (Dictionary.com)

Like the other laws, the Law of Polarity neither points out nor determines your choice of experience. It exists as a point of comparison so that you know what it means to live a fulfilled life. And if you address it with wisdom, you can learn to use it to your advantage.

You now know that the method of opposites helps you create the things you desire. In order to turn an existing situation into another—which is aligned with the desired effect—it is necessary to change the quality of the thought that first created the situation. The Law of Attraction, which states that you create all the situations in your life, works precisely on the basis of that understanding.

Accordingly, if you happen to come across a situation where you feel, for example, that you are being exploited by others, you have to look for the reason in the convictions you hold; and acknowledge them. Supposedly, your belief is: "If I do not always give in to the demands of others, I will be alone in life." It stands to reason that, in order to experience another result, you should first change that belief. To the question which belief could be more useful to you, the answer is: it depends on your model of the world. If you had said instead: "I respect myself and I set my own priorities", then that belief would certainly create a very different reality for you than the one you are experiencing today.

When you manage to fully understand the unwavering truth of this reality and accept personal responsibility for your choice—the choice of pole on the spectrum of polarity—you will have taken a significant step forward in achieving what we call know thyself and self-control. Self-awareness and self-control will guide you to the next step of evolution and to the life you want.

"IF ONLY THINGS WERE GOOD NOW..."

People often complain that it would be easier for them to concentrate on something positive, if only good things were already happening to them: if their relationship was better, their partner was more cooperative, their body did not ache, their work was emotionally fulfilling, or if the economic situation improved. The truth is that it is easier to feel good when you are experiencing situations that feel good. Nobody can deny that.

132

Nevertheless, if you believe that you are only able to concentrate on what is happening around you—which you find unpleasant—then you are at risk of prolonging your stay in that state of non-fulfillment. That is because your present focus—on the things you do not want—actually prevents the things you do want to come into your life.

It is also important to understand that you cannot be asking others to only create pleasant situations around you or for your sake. Clearly, it is not their responsibility. Other people can only control what they create for themselves; consistent with their personal vibrations and their own purpose in life. Most importantly, you should refrain from asking them, because it is not in your best interest. It is as if you are relinquishing your power; the power to create your own life experience the way you want to. It is, therefore, your responsibility to choose and shape the experiences that will guide you in the path of your goals in life.

Regardless of what you are currently experiencing, there is no need for you to wait for something good to happen in order to feel good, because you are always capable to direct your thoughts towards an improved situation.

As long as you care about how you feel and are willing to turn your attention to better thoughts, it will not be long before you set out to positively and deliberately transform your life.

THIS LAW AND OTHER LAWS

The Law of Attraction teaches us that no matter which vibration we send out, that is the vibration we will receive. In other words, the things that will come into your experience will come in response to your vibration. Accordingly, your vibration is the result of the thoughts you make. You can easily discern the nature of these thoughts from the emotions they produce. Look for good vibrational thoughts and a good vibrational creation will follow.

In short, in order to experience positive events, situations and circumstances, you have to focus on anything that is positive.

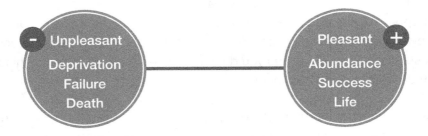

If you now accept something the way it is, consistent with the Law of "Allowing", you are on the opposite side of resistance: you are on the pole of acceptance. From that position, the things you do not want will gradually disappear.

Observe the contrast for a while, in order to gain clarity on what you do not want, and then take your focus away. For example, if you hear some bad news, observe the situation only for as long as it is necessary to form your desire for the contrary. Do not allow yourself to connect with the energy of shortage, poverty, deprivation, fear or destruction that this news might carry. You should, however, grant the people involved the right of personal choice. If you want you may offer to help, but do not engage in the situation with negative emotions.

Within the entire spectrum of the Law of Polarity there is pain and suffering, just as there is happiness, opportunity, and improvement. What actually determines the experience that someone will have, within this range, is his desire and choice.

Learn to accept that and express your sincere and heartfelt gratitude for whatever you are currently experiencing and you will soon realize that you are headed towards more positive situations.

CHOOSING YOUR TRUTH

Each event and each situation integrate opportunity and the possibility of the opposite experience.

The final outcome depends solely on your decision about which end of the spectrum you choose to experience. Between two apparently conflicting situations, the only determining factor is that which you consider to be possible and true.

It is very important to understand the power of the transformation that you can achieve when you apply the Law of Polarity. If you are willing to change your perception of a situation, this would mean that your attitude to life—resulting from that precise situation—would change simultaneously. It is true that you can change your perception of someone or something; from bad to good and from difficult to easy. And then, that new perception becomes your new reality.

When you are looking for a higher frequency vibration, through the deliberate change of your focus, the previous low frequency vibration gets replaced; because your body cannot emit two different vibrations at the same time. And that is a major step towards change. In our example, the bad (low vibration) reveals the manifestation of the good (high vibration). With that new perspective, you can become more efficient in managing situations. It is up to you, though, to make those choices, and change your perception and attitude towards situations. It is also up to you to choose the life that you want.

METAPHYSICAL AND PHYSICAL: THE POLES ON THE AXIS OF CREATION

Let us move on to yet another application of the law—the confrontation between the physical and the metaphysical world. The physical world consists of all things visible, anything that you can see, hear, touch, smell and taste. The metaphysical world is immaterial and comprises thoughts, feelings, emotions, and energy. To be able to create anything you want in your life, you must ensure that you harmoniously combine both planes: the physical and metaphysical.

Your metaphysical essence takes on the energy work required to prepare the ground for creation. That is to say, it is responsible for the alignment of thoughts, beliefs, and feelings with what you want to experience. After that, your physical essence assumes harmonious action so as to turn your desires into matter and experience.

Only through the combined and harmonious action of those two poles, can we create the things we want. Thought without action is not creation. Action without consistent thought signifies a difficult, painful and time-consuming creation.

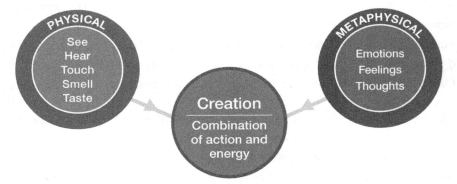

Harmony in thought and action leads to gratifying and evolutional creation. There are two prerequisites necessary for you to be able to create the things you want: you have to do energy work in the metaphysical world and undertake action in the physical world. However, if you start working on achieving your goals from the metaphysical part of the equation—via the application of the laws that are cited in this reading—not only will you get a head start, but also your action in the physical world will become easier and more enjoyable.

APPLYING THE LAW OF POLARITY

How can you experience the opposite of what displeases you? How can you develop the necessary belief, so as to experience the opposite of what you have in your life today?

You can, by way of education and experience. By reading these lines and then by experimenting with your everyday life. By observing yourself and discovering who you really are. By disproving false beliefs that oppose both your true nature and your unlimited power and by knowing yourself. And finally, by means of constantly and consistently practicing on the shift to the positive pole of things.

You have to fully understand the Law of Polarity to feel the joy, satisfaction, pleasure and prosperity that you so desire.

The Law of Polarity exists as a means to allow yourself to be extended and live life to the fullest. Practice and learn how to harmonize your thoughts, beliefs and actions with your aspirations; which will eventually lead you to a life of unconditional fulfillment.

Regardless of the experiences you have had so far, you have the ability and the potential to experience harmony and completeness in every field of your life.

You can, therefore, start by declaring your new intention and say: "Now, wherever I go, whatever I do, I intend to look for what I really want to see." Accept it and try to locate the positive aspects in things and situations and direct your attention to those alone. Look only for the things that make you feel good, sit back and observe how your life becomes more and more positive.

Even if you cannot be somewhere else than where you are right now, you always have the power to make your perspective known—express where you want to go and bring the change you want. In such a way, not only will your perception improve, but it will also keep on expanding. And given that your focus is conscious and deliberate, the results will be visible everywhere: on anything you turn your attention to.

Provided you understand and accept—without showing resistance—anything that comes along, you will make notable progress in shaping the particular life experience that you want.

Take a break and spend some time (maybe even a few days) to process the Law of Polarity and practice its application. The templates that you will find in the Workbook are designed to support you in your effort.

Chapter 8
ALL THE LAWS WORK TOGETHER

All the Laws of the Universe function in
an incessant, non discriminatory way and
in perfect harmony with one another, so
as to provide a life that is meaningful,
gratifying and evolutional.

All the Laws work together

In this book we presented you with the seven laws or the seven quantum principles whose comprehension and implementation leads to new paths of freedom, creation, recognition and completeness.

The operation of these laws is permanent and constant. These laws do not make exceptions. They neither judge, nor discriminate. Whether or not we are aware of their existence, they are valid and they affect the results in our lives. And those results are only contingent upon the conscious or unconscious application of the laws, by means of our individual action.

The laws relate to one another in an interactive and complementary fashion. Each law complements and reinforces the one that precedes, and all of them combined create an amazing operating system which sets in motion a universe of infinite possibilities. A universe that is designed to provide the basis for someone to build a life of creativity, cooperation, love, harmony and completeness. This is a possibility available to all without exception, as we are all made of the same energy: the energy of Well-being. Likewise, we all are privileged to access, in exactly the same way, the greatness of the physical dimension of life.

Now you know the rules of life, those who you were never taught by any educational, religious or cultural system, or even by the people of your immediate environment. All of this information concerning the principles that govern the universe is now part of your conscious mind. And with constant and consistent practice in applying them—as the common denominator—the eventual transition to a new path—a new reality is now made possible.

Now you know that, if you allow it, your thoughts can become your experience. Imagine yourself heading towards a future filled with love and faith, getting closer day by day. Free yourself from situations that derive from fear and stop recycling them. Recover your strength and your oppressed passion for life and creation, and get in touch with your true self that shines from its inner light.

You also know well that your dreams for the future are a possibility which is in your hands. And indeed, you have every reason to pursue them. Because you now understand that your energy, emanating from your spirit, will attract more energy of the same quality. And with that energy you will infuse everyone around you, in a constantly-expanding light wave. Moreover, you know that shriveling up does no one any good. On the contrary, when you manage to release your strength and live the abundant life that you want, both you and your environment are to benefit. For the mere reason that, you will then be able to offer more and to dynamically contribute to everyone's progress in creating an improved and more gratifying life.

Imagine a world where everyone knows and uses the laws. Visualize a place where your dreams, as well as the dreams of everyone else, come true. Life is but an amazing journey of experiences, discovery, learning, expansion and development. You are all aware of your connection with the infinite energy source of the universe. Knowing that abundance is your birthright, you consciously choose to be in this energy sphere. Since living in the sphere provides you with endless creative possibilities, you can—at any time—aspire to something new. You deliberately and consciously select that what you want to experience, you take action, and you allow things to unfold. In time and with a lot of practice, you will be able to maintain your focus on the positive pole of experiences and remain detached while creation forms; and that will eventually become a way of life for you. There will no longer be fear or doubt as to the outcome of situations, only peaceful anticipation and search for the knowledge that will lead to further expansion. The Law of Attraction works the same as always, only that now it delivers actions of high vibration which correspondingly give rise to new, higher vibrations and so on. And this amazing swirl of magnetic energy creation continues to move towards infinity, in an ascending path to new spheres of awareness, knowledge and experience.

Try to daily align your vibration with your desires, and go about it in a persistent and consistent way. When you obtain vibrational alignment, any action will appear to be inspirational. Without vibrational alignment, any action will seem difficult. With vibrational alignment, each one of your efforts will eventually bring the desired result. Without vibrational alignment, the outcome of your efforts will possibly be different from what you were expecting and you may get disappointed.

This likelihood might make you say, "These theories are not for me." But words like these are actually doubts of the Ego and, if you were to adhere to them, it stands to reason that you will remain trapped in the same situations. Because, if you once again indulge in these thoughts, you will basically deprive yourself of the opportunity to experience a different reality: one that is nearer to the harmony, the completeness, the peace and the Well-being you desire.

Accordingly, I propose–in view of every essential desire you have—to spend a few minutes of your time to check whether you are in alignment with the Laws of the Universe. To detect what thought, belief, or emotion is hiding behind your desire. Consider the laws and try to understand if you actually apply them or if there is something obstructing your efforts. Failure to apply any one of the rules will hinder the implementation of the others and will most likely prevent you from experiencing your desires in an empirical way. It, therefore, goes to show you that your efforts must be geared towards the implementation of all the laws; as in a daily, conscious system of activation and behavior.

This is a simple procedure which allows you to engage into action with more awareness, more consistency and ease in order to create the things you want. The more you practice, the more familiar you become with the application of laws and the more automatic the control procedure will be. You can look in the Workbook for the relevant exercise.

At this point, I suggest that you keep the following simple and comprehensive ideas, resulting from this reading, easily accessible so as to refer to them whenever you feel that you are in need of power and inspiration to move forward:

- All the experiences in your life are based on the energy vibration emanating from your thoughts, emotions, and actions.

- While you are choosing your thoughts, your emotions help you realize whether you are moving towards your desires or away from them.

- At any point in time, you know if your thoughts and actions obstruct or resist the current of Well-being, from the way that you are feeling.

- You have to practice on directing your mind to the location of your desires and not to the location of their absence or lack.

- Allow yourself to receive your desires by substituting thoughts of resistance and doubt with faith. Take life lightly and look for knowledge and pleasure in every experience.

- Refute your former limiting beliefs that make you weak and distance you from the life you are aspiring to have. Replace them with new empowering beliefs that will support you in whatever you do.

- When you are confused, first give yourself relief by changing the focus of you thought to something more positive. In short, let the current turn your boat downstream. Remember that action alone does not have enough power to compensate for the competitive energy of non-harmonious thoughts.

⊙—ᴨ Get to know, love and accept your true self. The rest will soon follow.

⊙—ᴨ Accept the diversity of others. Dismiss judgment and criticism, since they both conceal a deep fear. Understand and forgive.

⊙—ᴨ Get rid of the perfect images that can only cause great pain. Be happy about today and be excited about tomorrow.

⊙—ᴨ In every difficult situation, there is an inherent solution. Search for it. Do not worry about anything. The universe will take care of you.

⊙—ᴨ Gain awareness and organize your life and your actions based on the rules of the universe. Practice on applying them daily and see the changes in your life.

Provided you have understood the above, you are now in a position to use the below diagram: illustrating the process of deliberate and consistent creation.

Create that which you desire

① Declare your intention	② Think, focus, and pay attention on why you want something	③ Harmonize with your intention
⑥ Release any thought process that obstructs you	⑤ Keep your concentration on what you want, not what you are missing	④ Mentally focus on gratitude
⑦ Expect nothing but complete success	⑧ Assume action towards your goal	⑨ Your action must be consistent with your intention

Epilogue ————————————————————————

The information you have just read came to my attention in a humble way, and not in an ostentatious or glamorous manner. But I found this information to be of such importance, that I immediately set out to spread the word. It only took one seminar on the topic, to realize that I was actually right. People's response was incredible. Most of them even had the same reaction as I did; they felt as if they had found the missing piece of the puzzle.

At the time I began applying the laws and accessing deeper levels of awareness, my life changed fundamentally. I managed to become more aware of my thoughts and emotions, and I would be able to immediately notice even the slightest deviation from the path of Well-being, from the intense feeling of distress that would come over me. By taking the necessary remedial action, I can now offer myself relief and alignment within a few minutes; whereas, in the past, it would have taken me days, if not weeks. On a daily basis, I deliberately spend a little time observing the abundance around me and I steer myself to join this energy, as a way to overcome the old program of deprivation and narrowness.

By often repeating, "Well-being is my birthright", I feel that my life attitude changes, since I am neither asking for a free ride, nor am I looking for something that is intended only for the few. I simply claim what is mine and prepare myself to receive it. Knowing that there are no guarantees, only the ones that I make for myself, I am tearing down the walls, allowing my deepest desires to form on the basis of an action plan aiming at achieving my purpose in life. I observe the outcomes of events, since I know that my thoughts and emotions created them in the first place. I treat people with utmost love and understanding, knowing that—although everyone's path is different—we all do the best we can at any given moment. In the face of challenge, I remain calm and composed; searching for the lesson in disguise. Most days, I feel at peace with myself and I am confident that I am on the right path. One step at a time, I am slowly adding new desires to my aspirations.

I hope that you found the information of the book to be interesting and perhaps it reminded you of truths you always knew existed, but have never fully understood them or consciously applied them before.

I would suggest that you read it again, this time allowing for breaks between sections, to contemplate on examples from personal experience that confirm the existence of the laws and the way they respond to your own thoughts and actions; regardless of the nature (positive or negative) of those experiences. The awareness and acknowledgment of where you are, at this exact moment, is very important, because it determines how your life will evolve. Even if your motive for reading this book was simple curiosity, see it as an opportunity for review and redefinition.

Make time for yourself and make it your priority to get to know you and listen to what you want. Set new goals and focus on them with faith. If necessary, ask for help. Find people who are able to understand you and support you in your journey. That does not make you weak, it shows you are intelligent and empowering, and signifies your determination for change.

Look at the people around you; how many do you think are capable of being truly happy and are willing to go beyond conventional behaviors and superficial action? How many aspire to create a reality that goes beyond the social symbols of success? How many remain calm, exhibit genuine behaviors, feel confident and show faith that their lives are evolving in the direction they want? And how many people inspire you, because they radiate light and because their actions add value not only to their lives, but to the lives of others as well?

How many people, instead, go on living the same routines day in, day out? Leading a life that is designed to provide only for their basic or superficial needs and rewards them with just a few moments of real joy and pleasure? How many discuss over and over the difficulties they face in an attempt to get a sense of value, just because they endure? How many succumb to doubt and refuse to believe that there might be something more? And how many people are complacent about the things they see around them for the mere reason that those things are familiar and safe?

In which category do you belong or would like to belong, for that matter?

Imagine yourself one year, three years, and ten years from now. How will your life be then, if you continue to live as you do now? What would you have accomplished? Which experiences do you think would you have come your way? What would you say at the end of the journey: "I have lived like most people around me..." or "I have experienced a rich and abundant life, the way I intended!"

Open your mind to new fields of awareness. Open your mind to infinite possibilities and to your unlimited power and talents. Life is exciting for it is an endless journey of development and progress.

Believe in your ability that you can do anything and you will. You no longer have the excuse that you do not know how.

Why hasn't anyone told me?

The success factors we were never taught

THE WORKBOOK

WORKBOOK

This book of exercises aims to help you understand and apply the Laws of the Universe.

It seeks to direct your mind so that you gain awareness of your present situation and slowly begin to form a new frame of thought and action that will allow you to create a different reality—one that is closer to your pursuits.

I encourage you to take a comprehensive look at your life, starting from all major fields consecutively: Health and Body, Relationships, Career, Finances, and Spiritual Life. Later on, you can get into more detail working on sub - areas, like romance, sex, family, community, time, home, fun etc.

If you prefer, you can choose to work on one field at a time, practicing the range of exercises included in this book. When you complete the cycle, you move on to the next field and so on.

The exercises included herein may either seem too simple or too hard, depending on your present level of awareness, the extent of your resistance, and the degree to which you sabotage yourself. It is up to you, however, to discipline and convince yourself—with internal dialogue—to assist you in this effort to turn your life around.

In order to do so, I suggest that you have a daily routine where you spend 10 -15 minutes of your time being completely focused; preferably in the beginning of the day.

The workbook will help you structure a high quality thought. And, provided that you practice on that thought with consistence, you will come to realize that you are in fact changing: one step at a time. You will be surprised to see that your phobias and resistances are shrinking, while peacefulness and clarity are gaining ground.

WORKBOOK

You will feel generous with yourself and others. Your heart will open up like a luminous flower and you will find pleasure and joy in every little thing that happens to you. You will be amazed at how different your reaction is now to things that you used to find confusing or frustrating.

As your choices become more and more conscious, you will often be inclined to shift your attention to the empowering interpretation of the events presented to you.

Intellectual and spiritual development is a journey without end; a voyage of ascend to new spheres of possibilities that forever exist in in time and space.

Once you conquer a level, you will want to move on to the next. With that in mind, the use of the exercises never really stops. Because every time you set a new target, you start from the beginning: from the information on the very first page that provides you with the necessary methodology, as well as the inspiration to continue.

Enjoy every minute of the journey, because that is where the meaning of life is.

If you need any help with the exercises, please send us a note at info@ trueme.co.

I will also be very happy to read of your successes. In that way, you will be positively contributing to spreading this energy of light, while also inspiring others to take the leap themselves.

And as more people join in the process, we will be able to build up the energy potential that will enable us to create a different reality; a different world for ourselves, our children and future generations.

With lots of love,
Nicole Mantzikopoulou

GETTING TO DEEPLY KNOW YOUR PRESENT SELF

EXERCISE
01

ACKNOWLEDGE WHAT
YOU HAVE CREATED SO
FAR IN YOUR LIFE

Observe what is around you: objects, situations, and people. Take a note of the important milestones of your life—positive and negative. Recognize the reality you experience in each field separately.

Do you like what you see? Or would you rather have some things improve? While you do this exercise, bear in mind that your external reality—events and experiences—is a direct reflection of your internal reality: the thoughts that you have made up to this moment.

Health / Body

Personal & Family Relationships

Career / Profession

....
....
....
....
....

Finances

....
....
....
....
....

Social Interactions

....
....
....
....
....

Spirituality / Personal development

....
....
....
....
....

EXERCISE 02

WHICH ARE THE THOUGHTS THAT YOU HAVE MADE OR CONTINUE TO MAKE IN ORDER TO CREATE EVERYTHING THAT IS AROUND YOU?

Write them all down: positive and negative. Both categories can give you valuable messages as to how your life has developed so far.

POSITIVE THOUGHTS

Health / Body

Personal & Family Relationships

Career / Profession

Finances

Social Interactions

Spirituality / Personal development

EXERCISE 03

WHICH ARE THE THOUGHTS THAT YOU HAVE MADE OR CONTINUE TO MAKE IN ORDER TO CREATE EVERYTHING THAT IS AROUND YOU?

Write them all down: positive and negative. Both categories can give you valuable messages as to how your life has developed so far.

DEBILITATING THOUGHTS

Health / Body

Personal & Family Relationships

Career / Profession

Finances

Social Interactions

Spirituality / Personal development

Gain awareness and practice on the application of the Law of Attraction

EXERCISE
04

**OBSERVE YOURSELF FOR AN
ENTIRE WEEK AND MAKE NOTES
OF THE NEGATIVE THOUGHTS YOU
MAKE THROUGHOUT THIS TIME**

Become aware of the way that your mind operates. How often does it revolve around negative thoughts?

In case thoughts elude you, observe your emotions and, if those are unpleasant, look for the thought that created them. In that way, you will come to understand how you have used the Law of Attraction to date.

WHAT DO YOU WANT TO
EXPERIENCE IN YOUR LIFE?

An essential prerequisite for experiencing what you want is, first, to have clarity about it. Taking the necessary action to achieve your goal comes immediately after. In that manner, you can deliberately put your mind power to use for the pursuit of your desire.

Make a list of your desires in the pages that follow. Take 15 minutes every day in order to work on the list, making necessary changes and updates. Do not discount your desires; write them all down. You do not need to share that list with anyone.

Contemplate on your desires being fulfilled the moment you write them down. Try to tune in, as often as possible, to whatever emotion is generated by that thought (i.e. happiness, security, success, etc.)

Show patience for the things that have not yet manifested. Make sure that, little by little, you improve and enhance your vibration; as you come within reach of the vibration of your desire.

Health / Body

Career / Profession

....
....
....
....
....

Finances

....
....
....
....
....

Social Interactions

....
....
....
....
....

Spirituality / Personal development

....
....
....
....
....

EXERCISE
06

WHAT IS IT THAT HINDERS YOU FROM BECOMING WHO YOU WANT TO BE AND INTERFERES WITH GETTING WHAT YOU WANT?

Spend some time taking notes of your restrictive thoughts and beliefs which are hiding behind unproductive action or inaction, for that matter. Refrain from judging or analyzing them. To acknowledge those thoughts is the first step to change; bringing about a more desirable outcome in your life.

Health / Body

Personal & Family Relationships

Career / Profession

Finances

Social Interactions

Spirituality / Personal development

WHAT DOES IT TAKE TO ALIGN YOURSELF WITH WHAT YOU WANT: HOW CAN YOU WORK ON IT?

Begin today by thinking about ways to create more pleasant experiences for yourself. Write down the first ideas that pop up in your mind. Which are the beliefs that you must abandon— which are the ones that you must adopt?

What action should you take in order to consciously change your life?

Health / Body

Personal & Family Relationships

Career / Profession

....
....
....
....
....

Finances

....
....
....
....
....

Social Interactions

....
....
....
....
....

Spirituality / Personal development

....
....
....
....
....

Gain awareness
and practice on
the application
of the Law
of Deliberate
Creation

To have a clear understanding of how you have used the Law of Deliberate Creation up till today, think of the goals you have set and what you have accomplished so far: i.e. studying in a particular field, getting a job at the company of your choice, owning your dream car, taking a certain trip abroad, being married to the love of your life, having a family, etc.

Once you do that, think about what it is that you want to deliberately create in your life from now on. I suggest that you also make an estimate of the time you will need for things to take effect; making sure that this time frame is not only realistic, but also attainable and motivating. As is often the case, people tend to overestimate what they can do in one year, while they underestimate what they can accomplish in three.

Check to see how this exercise impacts you. How do you feel about the possibility to create anything that you want: happiness or doubt?

EXERCISE

08

THE GOALS YOU HAVE
ACCOMPLISHED SO FAR

Write down every success you have had; no matter how big or small. While you do that, let your feelings of happiness, satisfaction, pride and gratitude sweep you away.

As you fill the pages with your achievements, make sure to acknowledge your power and value.

Health / Body

Personal & Family Relationships

Career / Profession

Finances

Social Interactions

Spirituality / Personal development

EXERCISE
09

THE GOALS THAT YOU WOULD LIKE TO ACCOMPLISH IN THE IMMEDIATE FUTURE
(in days, weeks, or months)

This exercise is designed to help you practice, as often as you can, on shaping your intention. In that way, you will train your mind to knowingly seek ideas and actions that are consistent with what you want to create.

Observe yourself while you record your intentions. Are you excited or uncertain? Even if you are hesitant, go ahead and complete the exercise. For that alone, the written statement of your desire is the first step in eliminating doubt.

Health / Body

Personal & Family Relationships

Career / Profession

....
....
....
....
....

Finances

....
....
....
....
....

Social Interactions

....
....
....
....
....

Spirituality / Personal development

....
....
....
....
....

EXERCISE

10

GAIN CLARITY ON YOUR GOALS AND BECOME ACTIVATED

This next exercise is particularly important as it has a triple positive effect:

- Gives you clarity about your true desires

- Motivates you to go after what you want

- Alleviates all previous resistance and doubt (if any)

Prioritize the fields of your life and select the one which concerns you the most at this particular moment. In the lines numbered: 1, 2, 3, etc., write down all the objectives you want to accomplish. Make sure you positively state your goals; identifying what you want to attain, and not what you want to avoid.

When you finish, go back to the first objective and use the rows: a, b, c, etc. to write down all the reasons why you want to obtain it. Again, express yourself only in a positive way. Use as many pages as you like. As you note down the reasons, let yourself get carried away by the positive emotions that they generate.

Observe the change in your energy and motivation, once you have completed the exercise. Repeat the procedure for every field, whenever you feel the need.

My Health / My Body

What do I want to experience (1-6)? Why do I want to (a-e)?

1 ....

    (a) ....

    (b) ....

    (c) ....

    (d) ....

    (e) ....

2 ....

    (a) ....

    (b) ....

    (c) ....

    (d) ....

    (e) ....

3 ....

    (a) ....

    (b) ....

    (c) ....

    (d) ....

    (e) ....

My Health / My Body

What do I want to experience (1-6)? Why do I want to (a-e)?

4 _____

    (a) _____

    (b) _____

    (c) _____

    (d) _____

    (e) _____

5 _____

    (a) _____

    (b) _____

    (c) _____

    (d) _____

    (e) _____

6 _____

    (a) _____

    (b) _____

    (c) _____

    (d) _____

    (e) _____

Personal Relationships

What do I want to experience (1-6)? Why do I want to (a-e)?

1 ....

    (a) ....

    (b) ....

    (c) ....

    (d) ....

    (e) ....

2 ....

    (a) ....

    (b) ....

    (c) ....

    (d) ....

    (e) ....

3 ....

    (a) ....

    (b) ....

    (c) ....

    (d) ....

    (e) ....

Personal Relationships

What do I want to experience (1-6)? Why do I want to (a-e)?

4 --

(a) --

(b) --

(c) --

(d) --

(e) --

5 --

(a) --

(b) --

(c) --

(d) --

(e) --

6 --

(a) --

(b) --

(c) --

(d) --

(e) --

Family Relationships

What do I want to experience (1-6)? Why do I want to (a-e)?

1 --

(a) --

(b) --

(c) --

(d) --

(e) --

2 --

(a) --

(b) --

(c) --

(d) --

(e) --

3 --

(a) --

(b) --

(c) --

(d) --

(e) --

Family Relationships

What do I want to experience (1-6)? Why do I want to (a-e)?

4 --

(a) --

(b) --

(c) --

(d) --

(e) --

5 --

(a) --

(b) --

(c) --

(d) --

(e) --

6 --

(a) --

(b) --

(c) --

(d) --

(e) --

Career / Profession

What do I want to experience (1-6)? Why do I want to (a-e)?

1 _____

    (a) _____

    (b) _____

    (c) _____

    (d) _____

    (e) _____

2 _____

    (a) _____

    (b) _____

    (c) _____

    (d) _____

    (e) _____

3 _____

    (a) _____

    (b) _____

    (c) _____

    (d) _____

    (e) _____

Career / Profession

What do I want to experience (1-6)? Why do I want to (a-e)?

4 ....

    (a) ....

    (b) ....

    (c) ....

    (d) ....

    (e) ....

5 ....

    (a) ....

    (b) ....

    (c) ....

    (d) ....

    (e) ....

6 ....

    (a) ....

    (b) ....

    (c) ....

    (d) ....

    (e) ....

Finances

What do I want to experience (1-6)? Why do I want to (a-e)?

1 --

    (a) ---

    (b) ---

    (c) ---

    (d) ---

    (e) ---

2 --

    (a) ---

    (b) ---

    (c) ---

    (d) ---

    (e) ---

3 --

    (a) ---

    (b) ---

    (c) ---

    (d) ---

    (e) ---

Finances

What do I want to experience (1-6)? Why do I want to (a-e)?

4 ....

    (a) ....

    (b) ....

    (c) ....

    (d) ....

    (e) ....

5 ....

    (a) ....

    (b) ....

    (c) ....

    (d) ....

    (e) ....

6 ....

    (a) ....

    (b) ....

    (c) ....

    (d) ....

    (e) ....

Social Interactions

What do I want to experience (1-6)? Why do I want to (a-e)?

1 --

    (a) --

    (b) --

    (c) --

    (d) --

    (e) --

2 --

    (a) --

    (b) --

    (c) --

    (d) --

    (e) --

3 --

    (a) --

    (b) --

    (c) --

    (d) --

    (e) --

Social Interactions

What do I want to experience (1-6)? Why do I want to (a-e)?

4 --

(a) --

(b) --

(c) --

(d) --

(e) --

5 --

(a) --

(b) --

(c) --

(d) --

(e) --

6 --

(a) --

(b) --

(c) --

(d) --

(e) --

Personal Development / Spirituality

What do I want to experience (1-6)? Why do I want to (a-e)?

1 _____

    (a) _____

    (b) _____

    (c) _____

    (d) _____

    (e) _____

2 _____

    (a) _____

    (b) _____

    (c) _____

    (d) _____

    (e) _____

3 _____

    (a) _____

    (b) _____

    (c) _____

    (d) _____

    (e) _____

Personal Development / Spirituality

What do I want to experience (1-6)? Why do I want to (a-e)?

4 _____

(a) _____

(b) _____

(c) _____

(d) _____

(e) _____

5 _____

(a) _____

(b) _____

(c) _____

(d) _____

(e) _____

6 _____

(a) _____

(b) _____

(c) _____

(d) _____

(e) _____

Gain awareness
and practice on
the application
of the Law of
"Allowing"

DO YOU JUDGE OR PRESSURE OTHERS TO BE, ACCORDING TO YOUR STANDARDS, OR DO YOU ALLOW THEM TO BE WHO THEY ARE?

Reflect on your thoughts, your words, and your actions and record them. Who are the people that you accept? Who are the people that you reject? What type of situations, beliefs and behaviors do you condemn?

Try to get a grasp of the way you have applied the Law of "Allowing" to date.

EXERCISE 12

BECOME AWARE OF THE WAYS YOU EXHIBIT RESISTANCE AND FAIL TO ALLOW THE MANIFESTATION OF YOUR DESIRES

Write down every thought and behavior that indicates your resistance to the accomplishment of the goals you have set for yourself.

EXERCISE

13

MAKE A LIST OF ALTERNATIVES THAT CAN OFFER YOU RELIEF AT TIMES WHEN YOU FEEL CONFUSED OR WHEN YOU ARE NO LONGER ALIGNED WITH YOUR DESIRE

If you are overcome by negative feelings, you must first seek relief. Succeeding to do so indicates that you have reduced your resistance to that particular experience. And when you reduce resistance, it means that you are better prepared to take on productive and inspired action. The list below will support you in your effort. Which activities are most likely to serve as positive stimuli in your case: a friendly get-together, a stroll in the park, listening to a favorite song? Use as many pages as you like and make sure that you refer to this exercise whenever you feel the need.

1 --

2 --

3 --

4 --

5 --

6 --

7 --

The 7 Laws
of the Universe

8 ....

9 ....

10 ....

11 ....

12 ....

13 ....

14 ....

15 ....

16 ....

17 ....

18 ....

19 ....

20 ....

Gain awareness and practice on the application of the Law of Abundance

EXERCISE

14

ABUNDANCE IS EVERYONE'S BIRTHRIGHT. PRACTICE ON THAT THOUGHT TO MAKE IT FAMILIAR AND REALISTIC. LET YOUR MIND EMBRACE THE THOUGHT OF ABUNDANCE IN ORDER TO FURTHER ATTRACT IT.

Begin to appreciate all that you have and all that you are in a position to enjoy, just because you live and breathe.

Even in the absence of all material possessions, the experience of life is amazing.

Focus your attention on nature and on every single thing that stimulates your senses.

Concentrate on your magnificent body and take the time to visualize a hundred trillion cells bringing on the magic.

Savor happiness in your everyday life: in the sounds, the scents and the flavors. Recognize the pleasure you get from a morning cup of coffee, an expression of affection (a smile, a hug, a kiss), and being with family or friends.

Take 5 minutes every day to think about all those things. Try to coordinate with the emotions produced by those thoughts. You should feel rich, generous and grateful for every single moment.

DO YOU MOVE ALONGSIDE THE SPHERE OF ABUNDANCE OR DEPRIVATION?

Read the following phrases carefully. Give 1 point to every phrase that you accept as your own and count the points which aggregate in each column. Compare the two totals to assess your orientation. Reflect on the message you get.

The mindset of Abundance	The mindset of Deprivation
Focus on what is right	Focus on what is wrong
There is plenty...	There is not enough....
I suffice	I am insufficient
Cooperation and Inspiration	Competition
Abundance for everyone	I struggle to claim my share
I can create anything I want	I expect others to give me what I want
I connect with my inner self	I focus on the outside world
Money and possessions are the result of my present energy level	Money and possessions are the root causes of my problems
I create abundance with ease and grace	I create abundance with force and struggle
I have the creative energy to implement anything I want	I work hard and I force situations

The universe supports me ☐	The universe occasionally supports me ☐
I can have it all ☐	I cannot have everything ☐
No one is better and no one is worse ☐	Others are either better or worse than I am ☐
I am always looking for the solution ☐	I am always focusing on the problem ☐
Success has no limits ☐	There is always a limit to success ☐
I allow: myself to be all it can be ☐	I obsruct an important part of who I am ☐
I deserve to be appreciated ☐	I am not worthy and I must constantly prove myself ☐
There is no ceiling to what I can do ☐	There is a ceiling to what I can do ☐
Love ☐	Fear ☐
Worthiness and contribution ☐	Self-pity and criticism ☐
I admire and support ☐	I envy and frown upon ☐
I have desires ☐	I have no desires ☐
I am responsible for my life ☐	I do not take responsibility for my life ☐
My actions are inspired ☐	My actions are erratic and hasty ☐
Organized and motivated action ☐	Procrastination and obstruction of myself ☐
Abudance is my birth right ☐	Lack is my daily experience ☐

Score .... Score ....

EXERCISE 16

**BECOME AWARE OF THE
ABUNDANCE YOU ALREADY HAVE:
FEEL IT AND EXPRESS YOUR
GRATITUDE**

Take 5 minutes **every day** to express your appreciation for the things you enjoy in your life. Write down at least 5 things or events for which you are grateful or appreciative. In that way, you will be able to align with positive vibrations: easily and effectively. Since this is a cumulative exercise, it is really important that you perform it daily. Preferably, when you wake up in the morning or just before you turn in at night.

EXERCISE

17

WHAT WOULD HAPPEN IF YOU WERE TO ALIGN YOUR THOUGHTS WITH ABUNDANCE?

Reflect on the best thought you can possibly have and let it guide you in the direction of what you want to create in each field of your life. Note them on spaces 1-6. Then, try to identify the "essence" that you are seeking from these experiences (by essence we mean the ultimate emotion/feeling that you will gain as a result of getting the experience, i.e freedom, peace, success etc.) and capture them on points a-e.

My Health / My Body

What do I want to experience (1-6)? What is the essence I am seeking (a-e)?

1 _____

    (a) _____

    (b) _____

    (c) _____

    (d) _____

    (e) _____

2 _____

    (a) _____

    (b) _____

    (c) _____

    (d) _____

    (e) _____

3

(a)

(b)

(c)

(d)

(e)

4

(a)

(b)

(c)

(d)

(e)

5

(a)

(b)

(c)

(d)

(e)

6

(a)

(b)

(c)

(d)

(e)

Personal Relationships

What do I want to experience (1-6)? What is the essence I am seeking (a-e)?

1 --

    (a) --

    (b) --

    (c) --

    (d) --

    (e) --

2 --

    (a) --

    (b) --

    (c) --

    (d) --

    (e) --

3 --

    (a) --

    (b) --

    (c) --

    (d) --

    (e) --

Personal Relationships

What do I want to experience (1-6)? What is the essence I am seeking (a-e)?

4 --

(a) --

(b) --

(c) --

(d) --

(e) --

5 --

(a) --

(b) --

(c) --

(d) --

(e) --

6 --

(a) --

(b) --

(c) --

(d) --

(e) --

Family Relationships

What do I want to experience (1-6)? What is the essence I am seeking (a-e)?

1 ....

    (a) ....

    (b) ....

    (c) ....

    (d) ....

    (e) ....

2 ....

    (a) ....

    (b) ....

    (c) ....

    (d) ....

    (e) ....

3 ....

    (a) ....

    (b) ....

    (c) ....

    (d) ....

    (e) ....

Family Relationships

What do I want to experience (1-6)? What is the essence I am seeking (a-e)?

4
- (a)
- (b)
- (c)
- (d)
- (e)

5
- (a)
- (b)
- (c)
- (d)
- (e)

6
- (a)
- (b)
- (c)
- (d)
- (e)

Career / Profession

What do I want to experience (1-6)? What is the essence I am seeking (a-e)?

1 ....

    (a) ....

    (b) ....

    (c) ....

    (d) ....

    (e) ....

2 ....

    (a) ....

    (b) ....

    (c) ....

    (d) ....

    (e) ....

3 ....

    (a) ....

    (b) ....

    (c) ....

    (d) ....

    (e) ....

Career / Profession

What do I want to experience (1-6)? What is the essence I am seeking (a-e)?

4
- (a)
- (b)
- (c)
- (d)
- (e)

5
- (a)
- (b)
- (c)
- (d)
- (e)

6
- (a)
- (b)
- (c)
- (d)
- (e)

Finances

What do I want to experience (1-6)? What is the essence I am seeking (a-e)?

1 ....
    (a) ....
    (b) ....
    (c) ....
    (d) ....
    (e) ....

2 ....
    (a) ....
    (b) ....
    (c) ....
    (d) ....
    (e) ....

3 ....
    (a) ....
    (b) ....
    (c) ....
    (d) ....
    (e) ....

Finances

What do I want to experience (1-6)? What is the essence I am seeking (a-e)?

4 ....

    (a) ....

    (b) ....

    (c) ....

    (d) ....

    (e) ....

5 ....

    (a) ....

    (b) ....

    (c) ....

    (d) ....

    (e) ....

6 ....

    (a) ....

    (b) ....

    (c) ....

    (d) ....

    (e) ....

Social Interactions

What do I want to experience (1-6)? What is the essence I am seeking (a-e)?

1 ....

   (a) ....

   (b) ....

   (c) ....

   (d) ....

   (e) ....

2 ....

   (a) ....

   (b) ....

   (c) ....

   (d) ....

   (e) ....

3 ....

   (a) ....

   (b) ....

   (c) ....

   (d) ....

   (e) ....

Social Interactions

What do I want to experience (1-6)? What is the essence I am seeking (a-e)?

4 ....

    (a) ....

    (b) ....

    (c) ....

    (d) ....

    (e) ....

5 ....

    (a) ....

    (b) ....

    (c) ....

    (d) ....

    (e) ....

6 ....

    (a) ....

    (b) ....

    (c) ....

    (d) ....

    (e) ....

Personal Development / Spirituality

What do I want to experience (1-6)? What is the essence I am seeking (a-e)?

1 ....

    (a) ....

    (b) ....

    (c) ....

    (d) ....

    (e) ....

2 ....

    (a) ....

    (b) ....

    (c) ....

    (d) ....

    (e) ....

3 ....

    (a) ....

    (b) ....

    (c) ....

    (d) ....

    (e) ....

Personal Development / Spirituality

What do I want to experience (1-6)? What is the essence I am seeking (a-e)?

4

    (a) ---

    (b) ---

    (c) ---

    (d) ---

    (e) ---

5

    (a) ---

    (b) ---

    (c) ---

    (d) ---

    (e) ---

6

    (a) ---

    (b) ---

    (c) ---

    (d) ---

    (e) ---

Gain awareness
and practice on
the application
of the Law
of Pure
Potentiality

EXERCISE 18

MAKE A LIST OF ALL YOUR TALENTS, QUALITIES AND SKILLS

Take into consideration what others say about you and include those things in the list as well. You can revisit the list often in order to supply it with additional information; as you increasingly realize your greatness.

My wonderful self

EXERCISE 19

EMPOWERING AFFIRMATIONS TO PERCEIVE YOUR ENDLESS POSSIBILITIES

Choose one or as many as you like. If you prefer, you can create new affirmations using your own words. Place the affirmations' page somewhere where it is easily seen throughout the day, or make a note in your daily agenda to go through them once every morning. As time goes by, the systematic use of these affirmations will bring a noticeable change to your emotions.

- I am always capable of handling every situation that arises
- I love and accept myself—I am who I am
- My potential is infinite
- Day by day my life becomes more wonderful
- Life endorses me in every possible way
- With every passing day, I feel more secure
- I am in the process of making positive life changes
- The perfect job is looking for me and now we meet
- Opportunities are everywhere; choices are limitless
- I am now willing to let go to the infinite flow of Well-being
- Abundance is freely flowing within
- Life lavishly meets my needs
- The fastest way to health is to fill my mind with pleasant thoughts
- I love every cell of my body
- I attract love to my life and now I receive it
- I am amazing and everyone loves me

EXERCISE

20

**THE MAGIC BOX
OF POSSIBILITIES**

Find a box that you like or make one and decorate it as you prefer. Search for pictures and images that represent the things you want to experience in life and place them inside the box. While doing that, tune with the energy that emanates from the pictures and repeat to yourself: *"Whatever is inside this box, it is there on my account!"*

Whatever is inside this box,
it is there on my account!

Gain awareness
and practice on
the application
of the Law of
Detachment

EXERCISE

21

PRACTICE DETACHMENT AND CONQUER YOUR FREEDOM

For many of us, detachment seems like the most difficult step in the creation process. It not only requires a deep understanding of all the previous laws, but also an improved level of awareness; even a change in our state of mind.

The exercises below are designed to help you recognize the situations, the people or the objects to which you are completely attached. To help you realize which is the part of your current reality that, should it change, the thought alone terrifies you. And which is the part that, should it remain the same, it is upsetting. For the reason that, in both cases, your willingness to avoid unpleasant feelings makes you resort to constantly trying—to the point of exhaustion—to control everything.

When you become attached to something, how do you choose to act? What is the impact of your actions on yourself and others?

Once you realize that, you can decide to detach yourself. And when you succeed, you may automatically discard that enormous burden produced by discomfort, anxiety, fear, or other similar emotions.

That is when you regain your freedom. And that is when you are ready—at any given moment—to head for new creation.

My Health / My Body

What am I attached to? (1-6). What is the impact
of that attachment on myself and others? (a-e)

1 --

    (a) --

    (b) --

    (c) --

    (d) --

    (e) --

2 --

    (a) --

    (b) --

    (c) --

    (d) --

    (e) --

3 --

    (a) --

    (b) --

    (c) --

    (d) --

    (e) --

My Health / My Body

What am I attached to? (1-6). What is the impact
of that attachment on myself and others? (a-e)

4

(a) --

(b) --

(c) --

(d) --

(e) --

5

(a) --

(b) --

(c) --

(d) --

(e) --

6

(a) --

(b) --

(c) --

(d) --

(e) --

Personal Relationships

What am I attached to? (1-6). What is the impact
of that attachment on myself and others? (a-e)

1 ....

    (a) ....

    (b) ....

    (c) ....

    (d) ....

    (e) ....

2 ....

    (a) ....

    (b) ....

    (c) ....

    (d) ....

    (e) ....

3 ....

    (a) ....

    (b) ....

    (c) ....

    (d) ....

    (e) ....

Personal Relationships

What am I attached to? (1-6). What is the impact
of that attachment on myself and others? (a-e)

4

(a)

(b)

(c)

(d)

(e)

5

(a)

(b)

(c)

(d)

(e)

6

(a)

(b)

(c)

(d)

(e)

Family Relationships

What am I attached to? (1-6). What is the impact
of that attachment on myself and others? (a-e)

1 --

    (a) --

    (b) --

    (c) --

    (d) --

    (e) --

2 --

    (a) --

    (b) --

    (c) --

    (d) --

    (e) --

3 --

    (a) --

    (b) --

    (c) --

    (d) --

    (e) --

Family Relationships

What am I attached to? (1-6). What is the impact
of that attachment on myself and others? (a-e)

4 --

(a) --

(b) --

(c) --

(d) --

(e) --

5 --

(a) --

(b) --

(c) --

(d) --

(e) --

6 --

(a) --

(b) --

(c) --

(d) --

(e) --

Career / Profession

What am I attached to? (1-6). What is the impact
of that attachment on myself and others? (a-e)

1 ....

    (a) ....

    (b) ....

    (c) ....

    (d) ....

    (e) ....

2 ....

    (a) ....

    (b) ....

    (c) ....

    (d) ....

    (e) ....

3 ....

    (a) ....

    (b) ....

    (c) ....

    (d) ....

    (e) ....

Career / Profession

What am I attached to? (1-6). What is the impact
of that attachment on myself and others? (a-e)

4 --

(a) --

(b) --

(c) --

(d) --

(e) --

5 --

(a) --

(b) --

(c) --

(d) --

(e) --

6 --

(a) --

(b) --

(c) --

(d) --

(e) --

Finances

What am I attached to? (1-6). What is the impact
of that attachment on myself and others? (a-e)

1 ....

    (a) ....

    (b) ....

    (c) ....

    (d) ....

    (e) ....

2 ....

    (a) ....

    (b) ....

    (c) ....

    (d) ....

    (e) ....

3 ....

    (a) ....

    (b) ....

    (c) ....

    (d) ....

    (e) ....

Finances

What am I attached to? (1-6). What is the impact
of that attachment on myself and others? (a-e)

4
_____

(a) _____
(b) _____
(c) _____
(d) _____
(e) _____

5
_____

(a) _____
(b) _____
(c) _____
(d) _____
(e) _____

6
_____

(a) _____
(b) _____
(c) _____
(d) _____
(e) _____

Social Interactions

What am I attached to? (1-6). What is the impact
of that attachment on myself and others? (a-e)

1 --

    (a) --

    (b) --

    (c) --

    (d) --

    (e) --

2 --

    (a) --

    (b) --

    (c) --

    (d) --

    (e) --

3 --

    (a) --

    (b) --

    (c) --

    (d) --

    (e) --

Social Interactions

What am I attached to? (1-6). What is the impact
of that attachment on myself and others? (a-e)

4 --

(a) --

(b) --

(c) --

(d) --

(e) --

5 --

(a) --

(b) --

(c) --

(d) --

(e) --

6 --

(a) --

(b) --

(c) --

(d) --

(e) --

Personal Development / Spirituality

What am I attached to? (1-6). What is the impact
of that attachment on myself and others? (a-e)

1 ....

    (a) ....

    (b) ....

    (c) ....

    (d) ....

    (e) ....

2 ....

    (a) ....

    (b) ....

    (c) ....

    (d) ....

    (e) ....

3 ....

    (a) ....

    (b) ....

    (c) ....

    (d) ....

    (e) ....

Personal Development / Spirituality

What am I attached to? (1-6). What is the impact
of that attachment on myself and others? (a-e)

4

(a)

(b)

(c)

(d)

(e)

5

(a)

(b)

(c)

(d)

(e)

6

(a)

(b)

(c)

(d)

(e)

EXERCISE 22

WHICH PARTS OF YOUR LIFE OR PARTICULAR SITUATIONS ARE LIKELY TO BENEFIT FROM APPLYING THE LAW OF DETACHMENT, PROVIDED YOU SHOW TRUST AND BE OPEN TO A SLIM CHANCE OF UNCERTAINTY? WHAT WOULD YOU STAND TO GAIN?

My Health / My Body

In which situation I decide right now to practice detachment (1-6)? What will I gain (a-e)?

1 ....

(a) ....

(b) ....

(c) ....

(d) ....

(e) ....

2 ....

(a) ....

(b) ....

(c) ....

(d) ....

(e) ....

3

(a)

(b)

(c)

(d)

(e)

4

(a)

(b)

(c)

(d)

(e)

5

(a)

(b)

(c)

(d)

(e)

6

(a)

(b)

(c)

(d)

(e)

Personal Relationships

In which situation I decide right now to practice
detachment (1-6)? What will I gain (a-e)?

1 --

   (a) ----------------------------------

   (b) ----------------------------------

   (c) ----------------------------------

   (d) ----------------------------------

   (e) ----------------------------------

2 --

   (a) ----------------------------------

   (b) ----------------------------------

   (c) ----------------------------------

   (d) ----------------------------------

   (e) ----------------------------------

3 --

   (a) ----------------------------------

   (b) ----------------------------------

   (c) ----------------------------------

   (d) ----------------------------------

   (e) ----------------------------------

Personal Relationships

In which situation I decide right now to practice
detachment (1-6)? What will I gain (a-e)?

4

(a) --

(b) --

(c) --

(d) --

(e) --

5

(a) --

(b) --

(c) --

(d) --

(e) --

6

(a) --

(b) --

(c) --

(d) --

(e) --

Family Relationships

In which situation I decide right now to practice
detachment (1-6)? What will I gain (a-e)?

1 ....

    (a) ....

    (b) ....

    (c) ....

    (d) ....

    (e) ....

2 ....

    (a) ....

    (b) ....

    (c) ....

    (d) ....

    (e) ....

3 ....

    (a) ....

    (b) ....

    (c) ....

    (d) ....

    (e) ....

Family Relationships

In which situation I decide right now to practice
detachment (1-6)? What will I gain (a-e)?

4 --

    (a) --

    (b) --

    (c) --

    (d) --

    (e) --

5 --

    (a) --

    (b) --

    (c) --

    (d) --

    (e) --

6 --

    (a) --

    (b) --

    (c) --

    (d) --

    (e) --

Career / Profession

In which situation I decide right now to practice
detachment (1-6)? What will I gain (a-e)?

1 ....

   (a) ....
   (b) ....
   (c) ....
   (d) ....
   (e) ....

2 ....

   (a) ....
   (b) ....
   (c) ....
   (d) ....
   (e) ....

3 ....

   (a) ....
   (b) ....
   (c) ....
   (d) ....
   (e) ....

Career / Profession

In which situation I decide right now to practice
detachment (1-6)? What will I gain (a-e)?

4 --

(a) --
(b) --
(c) --
(d) --
(e) --

5 --

(a) --
(b) --
(c) --
(d) --
(e) --

6 --

(a) --
(b) --
(c) --
(d) --
(e) --

Finances

In which situation I decide right now to practice
detachment (1-6)? What will I gain (a-e)?

1 _____

(a) _____

(b) _____

(c) _____

(d) _____

(e) _____

2 _____

(a) _____

(b) _____

(c) _____

(d) _____

(e) _____

3 _____

(a) _____

(b) _____

(c) _____

(d) _____

(e) _____

Finances

In which situation I decide right now to practice
detachment (1-6)? What will I gain (a-e)?

4

   (a)

   (b)

   (c)

   (d)

   (e)

5

   (a)

   (b)

   (c)

   (d)

   (e)

6

   (a)

   (b)

   (c)

   (d)

   (e)

Social Interactions

In which situation I decide right now to practice
detachment (1-6)? What will I gain (a-e)?

1 ....

(a) ....

(b) ....

(c) ....

(d) ....

(e) ....

2 ....

(a) ....

(b) ....

(c) ....

(d) ....

(e) ....

3 ....

(a) ....

(b) ....

(c) ....

(d) ....

(e) ....

Social Interactions

In which situation I decide right now to practice
detachment (1-6)? What will I gain (a-e)?

4
(a)
(b)
(c)
(d)
(e)

5
(a)
(b)
(c)
(d)
(e)

6
(a)
(b)
(c)
(d)
(e)

Personal Development / Spirituality

In which situation I decide right now to practice
detachment (1-6)? What will I gain (a-e)?

1 ....

(a) ....

(b) ....

(c) ....

(d) ....

(e) ....

2 ....

(a) ....

(b) ....

(c) ....

(d) ....

(e) ....

3 ....

(a) ....

(b) ....

(c) ....

(d) ....

(e) ....

Personal Development / Spirituality

In which situation I decide right now to practice
detachment (1-6)? What will I gain (a-e)?

4 --

   (a) --

   (b) --

   (c) --

   (d) --

   (e) --

5 --

   (a) --

   (b) --

   (c) --

   (d) --

   (e) --

6 --

   (a) --

   (b) --

   (c) --

   (d) --

   (e) --

Gain
awareness
and practice on
the application
of the Law
of Polarity

EXERCISE

23

THE LAW OF POLARITY
IS THE MOST STRAIGHT-FORWARD
LAW AND ONE OF THE EASIEST
TO APPLY

In general, when we are faced with an unwanted experience, we are more than capable of expressing what we want instead. And so, through practice, it becomes easier for us to remain on the axis of our desires and not the lack thereof.

The exercises which are given here are designed to help you achieve precisely that. Choose the one that suits you best or use them all, for that matter. The result you will achieve is that you will be able to maintain your focus on the positive end. That will not only grant you energy and motivation, but it will also give you even greater clarity concerning the things that you can accomplish.

Enhance your perception of situations that you find troublesome. Every situation and circumstance in your life can improve. But you have to realize in which areas your focus stays on the negative side of the axis. Can you assign a different meaning to the things that worry you? Now is the time to look for a better interpretation.

My Health / My Body

What am I concerned about(1-6)? What other meaning(s)
can I assign to it, to feel better, or even more empowered (a-e)?

1 ....

    (a) ....

    (b) ....

    (c) ....

    (d) ....

    (e) ....

2 ....

    (a) ....

    (b) ....

    (c) ....

    (d) ....

    (e) ....

3 ....

    (a) ....

    (b) ....

    (c) ....

    (d) ....

    (e) ....

My Health / My Body

What am I concerned about(1-6)? What other meaning(s)
can I assign to it, to feel better, or even more empowered (a-e)?

4 --

    (a) --

    (b) --

    (c) --

    (d) --

    (e) --

5 --

    (a) --

    (b) --

    (c) --

    (d) --

    (e) --

6 --

    (a) --

    (b) --

    (c) --

    (d) --

    (e) --

Personal Relationships

What am I concerned about(1-6)? What other meaning(s)
can I assign to it, to feel better, or even more empowered (a-e)?

1 ....

    (a) ....

    (b) ....

    (c) ....

    (d) ....

    (e) ....

2 ....

    (a) ....

    (b) ....

    (c) ....

    (d) ....

    (e) ....

3 ....

    (a) ....

    (b) ....

    (c) ....

    (d) ....

    (e) ....

Personal Relationships

What am I concerned about(1-6)? What other meaning(s)
can I assign to it, to feel better, or even more empowered (a-e)?

4 ....

    (a) ....

    (b) ....

    (c) ....

    (d) ....

    (e) ....

5 ....

    (a) ....

    (b) ....

    (c) ....

    (d) ....

    (e) ....

6 ....

    (a) ....

    (b) ....

    (c) ....

    (d) ....

    (e) ....

Family Relationships

What am I concerned about(1-6)? What other meaning(s)
can I assign to it, to feel better, or even more empowered (a-e)?

1 _____

    (a) _____

    (b) _____

    (c) _____

    (d) _____

    (e) _____

2 _____

    (a) _____

    (b) _____

    (c) _____

    (d) _____

    (e) _____

3 _____

    (a) _____

    (b) _____

    (c) _____

    (d) _____

    (e) _____

Family Relationships

What am I concerned about(1-6)? What other meaning(s)
can I assign to it, to feel better, or even more empowered (a-e)?

4 --

(a) --

(b) --

(c) --

(d) --

(e) --

5 --

(a) --

(b) --

(c) --

(d) --

(e) --

6 --

(a) --

(b) --

(c) --

(d) --

(e) --

Career / Profession

What am I concerned about(1-6)? What other meaning(s)
can I assign to it, to feel better, or even more empowered (a-e)?

1 _____

    (a) _____

    (b) _____

    (c) _____

    (d) _____

    (e) _____

2 _____

    (a) _____

    (b) _____

    (c) _____

    (d) _____

    (e) _____

3 _____

    (a) _____

    (b) _____

    (c) _____

    (d) _____

    (e) _____

Career / Profession

What am I concerned about(1-6)? What other meaning(s)
can I assign to it, to feel better, or even more empowered (a-e)?

4 --

    (a) --

    (b) --

    (c) --

    (d) --

    (e) --

5 --

    (a) --

    (b) --

    (c) --

    (d) --

    (e) --

6 --

    (a) --

    (b) --

    (c) --

    (d) --

    (e) --

Finances

What am I concerned about(1-6)? What other meaning(s)
can I assign to it, to feel better, or even more empowered (a-e)?

1 _____

   (a) _____
   (b) _____
   (c) _____
   (d) _____
   (e) _____

2 _____

   (a) _____
   (b) _____
   (c) _____
   (d) _____
   (e) _____

3 _____

   (a) _____
   (b) _____
   (c) _____
   (d) _____
   (e) _____

Finances

What am I concerned about(1-6)? What other meaning(s)
can I assign to it, to feel better, or even more empowered (a-e)?

4 ....

    (a) ....

    (b) ....

    (c) ....

    (d) ....

    (e) ....

5 ....

    (a) ....

    (b) ....

    (c) ....

    (d) ....

    (e) ....

6 ....

    (a) ....

    (b) ....

    (c) ....

    (d) ....

    (e) ....

Social Interactions

What am I concerned about(1-6)? What other meaning(s)
can I assign to it, to feel better, or even more empowered (a-e)?

1 ....

    (a) ....

    (b) ....

    (c) ....

    (d) ....

    (e) ....

2 ....

    (a) ....

    (b) ....

    (c) ....

    (d) ....

    (e) ....

3 ....

    (a) ....

    (b) ....

    (c) ....

    (d) ....

    (e) ....

Social Interactions

What am I concerned about(1-6)? What other meaning(s)
can I assign to it, to feel better, or even more empowered (a-e)?

4 --

(a) --

(b) --

(c) --

(d) --

(e) --

5 --

(a) --

(b) --

(c) --

(d) --

(e) --

6 --

(a) --

(b) --

(c) --

(d) --

(e) --

Personal Development / Spirituality

What am I concerned about(1-6)? What other meaning(s)
can I assign to it, to feel better, or even more empowered (a-e)?

1 ....
- (a) ....
- (b) ....
- (c) ....
- (d) ....
- (e) ....

2 ....
- (a) ....
- (b) ....
- (c) ....
- (d) ....
- (e) ....

3 ....
- (a) ....
- (b) ....
- (c) ....
- (d) ....
- (e) ....

Personal Development / Spirituality

What am I concerned about(1-6)? What other meaning(s)
can I assign to it, to feel better, or even more empowered (a-e)?

4 --

(a) --

(b) --

(c) --

(d) --

(e) --

5 --

(a) --

(b) --

(c) --

(d) --

(e) --

6 --

(a) --

(b) --

(c) --

(d) --

(e) --

EXERCISE 24

GAIN CLARITY ON ANYTHING THAT TROUBLES YOU AND CONCENTRATE ON ITS SOLUTION

Based on a tool by Law of Attraction teacher Michael Losier,
www.LawofAttractionBook.com

The following exercise is very powerful. In just a short period of time, it can help you get a different, empowering perspective on those situations or parts of your life that concern you. It will also give you clarity and you will come to realize how you can benefit from concentrating on your desires.

In the left column, which is marked "Issue", list the things that worry you with regard to the various areas of your life. Make an effort to leave no blanks. If needed, you may use an additional sheet.

When you have completed the list, go back to the first point you have made. As you read it, reflect on what you would like to experience now, in comparison. Mark that down in the column of "Desire", just opposite the point that troubles you. Make sure that your tone is positive. Also, you have to express it in the form of a statement and not as a wish.

As soon as you write it, turn to your initial point of concern and cross it out.

Repeat the process for the remaining points.

After you finish, fold the page so that you can only see the list of Desires. Read the list out loud; trying to infuse your words with emotions. Can you feel your power rising?

Keep the list within reach so that you can revisit it as often as you like.

Perform that process every time you feel confused about a situation or are in need of a better perspective.

My Health / My Body

Issue

Write here the things you dislike or worry about regarding this particular field.

01. Example: I don't want to be fat
02.
03.
04.
05.
06.
07.
08.
09.
10.

Desire

Write here what you want to experience contrary to your concern. Express yourself positively.

01. I return to my perfect weight
02.
03.
04.
05.
06.
07.
08.
09.
10.

Personal Relationships

Issue

Write here the things
you dislike or worry
about regarding this
particular field.

01. Example: I do not want to fight
with my partner
02. ....
03. ....
04. ....
05. ....
06. ....
07. ....
08. ....
09. ....
10. ....

Desire

Write here what you want
to experience contrary
to your concern. Express
yourself positively.

01. I am in a harmonious relationship
with my partner
02. ....
03. ....
04. ....
05. ....
06. ....
07. ....
08. ....
09. ....
10. ....

Career / Profession

Issue

Write here the things you dislike or worry about regarding this particular field.

01. Example: My job oppresses me
02. ....
03. ....
04. ....
05. ....
06. ....
07. ....
08. ....
09. ....
10. ....

Desire

Write here what you want to experience contrary to your concern. Express yourself positively.

01. I have an interesting job that develops me
02. ....
03. ....
04. ....
05. ....
06. ....
07. ....
08. ....
09. ....
10. ....

Finances

Issue	Desire
Write here the things you dislike or worry about regarding this particular field.	Write here what you want to experience contrary to your concern. Express yourself positively.

Issue

01. Example: I do not want to be in debt
02.
03.
04.
05.
06.
07.
08.
09.
10.

Desire

01. I have all my financial affairs in order
02.
03.
04.
05.
06.
07.
08.
09.
10.

Social Interactions

Issue

Write here the things you dislike or worry about regarding this particular field.

01. Example: People misunderstand me
02. ....
03. ....
04. ....
05. ....
06. ....
07. ....
08. ....
09. ....
10. ....

Desire

Write here what you want to experience contrary to your concern. Express yourself positively.

01. People around me get my good intentions
02. ....
03. ....
04. ....
05. ....
06. ....
07. ....
08. ....
09. ....
10. ....

Personal development / Spirituality

Issue

Write here the things you dislike or worry about regarding this particular field.

01. Example: I am stuck on the same routine
02. ....
03. ....
04. ....
05. ....
06. ....
07. ....
08. ....
09. ....
10. ....

Desire

Write here what you want to experience contrary to your concern. Express yourself positively.

01. Every experience in my life makes me grow
02. ....
03. ....
04. ....
05. ....
06. ....
07. ....
08. ....
09. ....
10. ....

EXERCISE

25

THE FOCUS WHEEL

A tool by Jerry & Esther Hicks, from the book "Ask and it is Given", 2010,AbrahamHicks.com

The exercise below is a quick and fun way to shift your focus towards the positive axis of things.

When you are preoccupied with something you do not like, think about what you would rather have instead. Write down, in the center of the wheel, what it is that you want.

Now indulge in the thought of the wheel rotating with the energy of your desire. While your focus is on the center—reading what you have written—look for an affirmation that matches your desire. In other words, think about what you stand to gain when your desire is met.

If that thought is invigorating, make a note of it in the space that corresponds to the upright position: position number 12 (as in the 12th hour of the clock). If, however, you have doubts, you should not put it down. In that case, you should keep looking for an affirmation that you believe in. The moment you find one, write it.

Keep looking for positive thoughts resulting from the fulfillment of your desire. Continue the process, until each of the remaining 11 positions is filled. Write additional affirmations on the external perimeter of the wheel; using up all the space.

Once you finish, you will be able to appreciate the change in your thinking and your energy output, with regard to your original concern. You can now take action prompted by enhanced motivation.

The 7 Laws of the Universe

The Focus Wheel

Example

Issue: I never have enough money

Desire: I have abundance in money

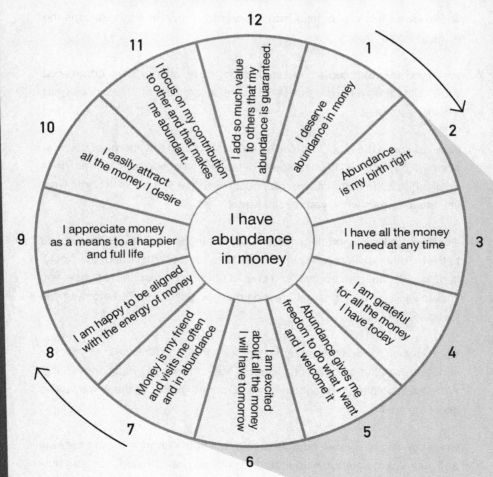

The Focus Wheel

Issue:
Desire:

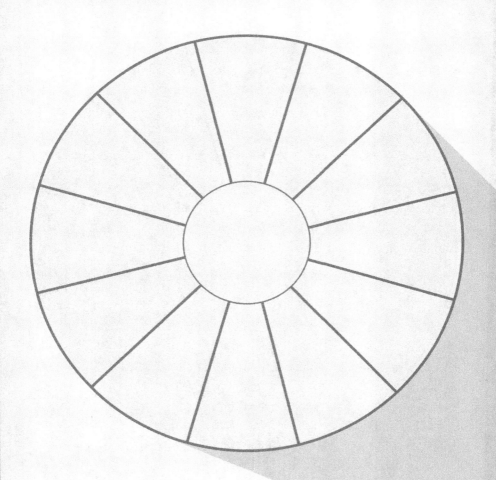

The Focus Wheel

Issue:

Desire:

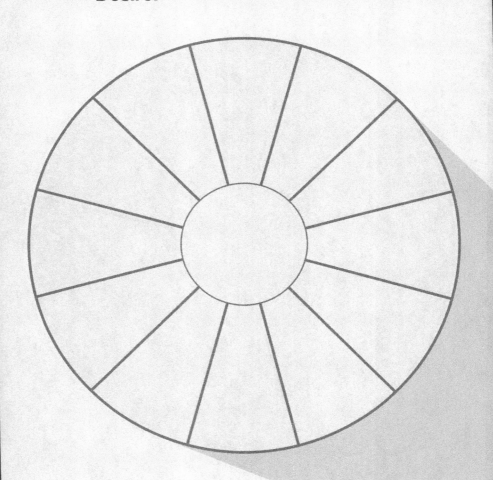

Making
the Laws
work
together

EXERCISE

26

ALL THE LAWS WORK TOGETHER

**PRACTICE ON APPLYING THEM
SIMULTANEOUSLY IN ORDER TO
GET DESIRED RESULTS**

By the time you reach this page, you will have acquired a sufficient level of self-awareness and understanding of your current situation, as well as your challenges and aspirations.

While in the process of setting new goals, practice on the application of the Laws to support yourself in achieving them. As you gain an overall perspective of things and provided that you simultaneously apply the Laws, you will experience an amazing head start to your pursuits.

To that end, use the following page to record your progress, your thoughts, challenges and victories; as you conquer new levels of thinking and action.

I wish you an enjoyable journey!

EXERCISE 26

ALL THE LAWS WORK TOGETHER
PRACTICE ON APPLYING THEM SIMULTANEOUSLY IN ORDER TO GET DESIRED RESULTS

The Law of Attraction
What resembles Self will attract Self

The Law of Deliberate Creation
That what you are consistently thinking and feeling you receive

The Law of "Allowing"
The principles of acceptance and non-resistance
Accepting myself
Accepting others
Releasing all resistance

The Law of Polarity
Everything has two poles that are equal and opposite
That guides us in shaping our desires

All the Laws work together

The Law of Abundance
We live in an abundant universe
Abundance is our birthright
You are abundance

The Law of Detachment
In order to be able to attain anything in the physical Universe you have to let go of your attachment to it

The Law of Pure Potentiality
Everything is possible
You can have access to infinite creativity when guided by your Spirit

I accomplish my goals

[By applying the Laws]

Goal:

Place a ✓ in whichever Law you apply to check your progress. State how you apply it.

1 Law of Attraction _____ ◯

_____

_____

_____

_____

2 Law of Deliberate Creation _____ ◯

_____

_____

_____

_____

3 Law of "Allowing" _____ ◯

_____

_____

_____

_____

4 Law of Abundance ⚪

---

5 Law of Pure Potentiality ⚪

---

6 Law of Detachment ⚪

---

7 Law of Polarity ⚪

BIBLIOGRAPHY

Hicks, Jerry and Esther Hicks. Ask and it is Given. Hay House, 2010. Print.

Arntz,William, Betsy Chasse, and Mark Vincente. What the Bleep Do We Know!?: Discovering the Endless Possibilities for Altering Your Everyday Reality. HCI; Mti edition, 2007. Print.

Kaku, Michio, and Jennifer Trainer Thompson. Beyond Einstein: The Cosmic Quest for the Theory of the Universe. Anchor; Rev Upd Su edition, 1995. Print.

Friedman,Norman.Bridging Science and Spirit: Common Elements in David Bohm's Physics, the Perennial Philosophy and Seth. Moment Point Press Inc; Reissue edition, 1997. Print.

Holmes, Ernest. The Science of Mind: A Philosophy, A Faith, A Way of Life. Tarcher Putnam, 1998. Print.

Lederman, Leon. The God Particle: If the Universe Is the Answer, What Is the Question?

Mariner Books; Reprint edition, 2006. Print.

Cole-Whittaker, Terry. What You Think Of Me Is None Of My Business. Jove; Reprint edition, 1988. Print.

Chopra, Deepak. The Seven Spiritual Laws of Success: A Practical Guide to the Fulfillment of Your Dreams. Amber-Allen Publishing, 2011. Print.

NOTES

NOTES

NOTES

# About the Author

Nicole Mantzikopoulou was born in Caracas Venezuela, where she spent her childhood and first teenage years. At the age of 14 her family moved back to its country of origin, Greece.

Nicole studied Business Administration in Athens and acquired her Master in Business Administration (MBA) in the UK.

During the first 24 years of her career Nicole became a highly successful business person, working in Fortune 100 multinational companies, in very high profile positions with global scope responsibilities. Nicole was reckoned for designing and implementing successful strategies, turning around businesses and leading organizations to growth. During these years, she had had the opportunity to meet hundreds of people, most of them leading demanding careers, overstressed, overworked and with no connection to their true life desires and goals.

In 2011, stemming from her own need for self-discovery, peace of mind, gratification and joy, Nicole decided to put her talents to help people set their own strategies for successful living.

Today, Nicole is the founder and CEO of the True-me® Breakthrough Coaching Company, specializing in Executive & Business Coaching as well as teens and Young Adults. She is a certified Master Coach in Neuro Linguistic Programming, Time Line Therapy & Hypnosis, A Quantum Success Coaching Academy Certified Coach, Emotional Freedom Techniques Practitioner, Member of The International Coaching Federation (ICF), Co-founder of the ICF Greek Chapter, Teaching Partner with The American College of Athens for its Adults Education Program.

Printed in the United States
By Bookmasters